THE SIMPLE SECRETS OF THE POWER TO HEAL

*How to treat
many persistent conditions
still defying conventional medicine.*

The Personal Opinions
of John Howard

A PRACTICAL GUIDE TO DRUG, DIET AND EXERCISE FREE NATURAL SELF-HEALING.

ONE OF THE GREATEST MEDICAL BREAKTHROUGHS OF ALL TIME

PLEASE NOTE

Prior to the use of the healing described in the book, it is essential that those to be treated consult their Doctor and any Specialist treating them. *This book is not in lieu of conventional medicine and medical advice.*

First published in August 1997

Published by Brindley Press
19-20 St. George's Avenue
Northamptonshire NN2 6JA

ISBN 0 9531435 0 3

Printed by Candor Print, Northampton.

THE SIMPLE SECRETS OF THE POWER TO HEAL

CONTENTS

PART THREE

AN INTRODUCTION TO HEALING

PART FOUR

ARTHRITIC CONDITIONS AND TREATMENT METHODS

PART FIVE

LIMB AND BODILY HEALING

PART SIX

STROKES AND CANCERS

PART SEVEN

FURTHER HEALING METHODS

PART EIGHT

TREATING MIND CONDITIONS

PART NINE

MAGNET THERAPY

FORWARD

In this book the concept and practice of Natural Healing is explained, but as befits such a healing process, in a way as free of technical terms as possible, and hopefully in an interesting and informative way. Some medical terms do occur but mostly to identify some bodily part, enabling the reader to pursue more in depth studies should they wish to.

However, should the reader seek a deeper insight there is a risk. This risk can be illustrated rather well by considering the bumble bee. Aerodynamically, we are told, it cannot fly. Happily, the bee being unaware of this 'fact' continues to fly. As with the bee so to is it with many aspects of natural healing, and from a traditional medical point-of-view much of it is technically impossible. The reader then, in studying medical text books is likely to realise the impossibility of such healing for himself, bringing with it the end of the healing project, or at least be likely to reduce its effectiveness.

I am reminded of a story I once heard years ago. A man applied for a life insurance sales post on a commission only basis. Anxious to recruit the enthusiastic applicant the local area manager painted a glowing prospect of the earning potential. Having told him of the high commission he would receive on each sale - which would equal his previous earnings for a fortnight's full time employment, the Area Manager then staggered the applicant by multiplying the commission amount by six, saying, "As you see, for only one sale a day you'll make as much in a week as you did in the three months before, and that's all you need to do, sell one policy a day - and that's what we expect our salesmen to do." In the first two weeks the applicant sold thirteen such policies.

On the Monday morning of his third week he was called to a Branch meeting. Having introduced himself to the others as a new member of the sales team, the others asked him how he was getting on, and he replied:
"O.K. I'm a bit above target".
"What target?" asked one.
"A policy sold every working day." He replied.
"What!" They responded. "A policy sold every working day?"

"Yes", He said "That's the normal target isn't it?"
"The normal target?" They replied, we think we're lucky to sell one policy each week - and that can take some doing."
Dismay and a sense of foolishness hit the new salesman, who's sales now also fell to one policy each week.

No, we are not to be concerned with hard medical facts, but with natural healing which can frequently bring spectacular results. It is because conventional medicine sticks strictly to tradition, and often has to of course, that so many health conditions continue on a vast scale - afflicting millions and millions of people, or with such conditions often only responding with fleeting relief to expensive drugs. Consequently, millions of people are faced with the prospect of having to use drugs for life! In their quest for a drug solution of arthritis, for instance, untold millions of pounds have been invested, yet still no cure has been discovered.

If you seek to discover some remedy, and do so by looking in to the wrong area, then that remedy cannot be found, and if such research is dominated or restricted by convention, then even realising the area for research is the wrong one becomes impossible.

For arthritis the answer is commonly to be found in the mind, and not in the affected bodily part. That is not to say the condition is imagined, but rather that the mind is the root to relief by encouraging it to bring about the healing. No matter how expensive or exotic then the drug, a drug aimed at treating the condition, while ignoring the consideration of the true location for healing cannot be expected to work. Hence the vast investments with little or nothing to show for the money and talents employed.

Research into Natural Healing is hardly undertaken. Yet for most of our history we survived without conventional medicine, and during that time we relied far more on our Natural Healing abilities, most of which have 'gone-by-the-board' today. Take, for instance, the way we sigh at given events, or often say 'Oh blow it!' These spontaneous reactions are like echoes from our self-healing of the past, and knowing this they can be developed and brought into effect, often with astounding results.

Then too, notice how often people repeatedly tap their own heads or repeatedly click their fingers when trying to remember some name or details. The use of this natural beneficial self-aid will be explained later in this work, and be shown to be able to produce the most amazing effects.

As a further example it is a natural response for us to hold some bodily part

- the hand held on the head for a headache, the hand on the stomach when it aches, or the elbow cradled by the hand of the other arm when the elbow has been knocked. But why? No research establishment that I have heard of has investigated this natural reaction to ask why we do it. Yet here the reader will learn how astonishing healing successes can be achieved by using 'hands-on' healing.

As a further example, how often do we encounter people who smilingly or laughingly report some personal misfortune or embarrassing situation? Yet here too is to be found a magical healing method, and one often producing astounding results.

A REMINISCENCE

In the autumn of 1946, when I was eight-years-old, we moved into a modern home. For the first time we actually had a real bathroom - no more tin baths by the fire, trips to an outside toilet or chamber pots under the bed. All-in-all a welcome and marvellous change. On visiting the bathroom from time-to-time during the night, I was alarmed and saddened on occasions to see blood stained 'bandages' in the washbasin, left there to soak.

Somehow, but I don't know why, I connected them with my mother. She was clearly very ill and her illness was making her bleed a lot. I never mentioned my enormous concern to her, and she seemed brave enough to pretend to be well. Despite her clever acting though I saw through it, and became increasingly afraid. It was only to be many years later, as I continued to ponder over the mystery, that I realised what I had been witnessing.

In the years immediately following the Second World War everything was scarce, and most things were still rationed. Added to this, my stepfather-to-be, held only a poorly paid job on the railways. What my mother had been doing in the bathroom all those years ago was just one of the things which she had to do to cope. However, with the experiences being repeated they instilled in me a dream, that I would grow up and one day discover some great universal healing remedy.

At first I had no idea what that remedy would be, but it would be something that made everyone well, and no matter what was wrong with them. Since the only treatment I had been given for illness came from a medicine bottle, it was obvious to me that my remedy had to be a bottled potion too, but a magical one. I knew nothing of science or medicine, and I couldn't wait to grow up for the 'emergency' already existed.

Something had to be done now! I realised that my only recourse was to begin experimenting immediately, there was no time to be lost. Everything had to be tried, no avenue of exploration could be ignored. I was spurred on in my enthusiasm by the unknown mother who, by using similar research methods, had discovered the bottle her husband used to oil the small caster wheels on his furniture, was also 'extremely good for small boys'. Whilst I always regretted that she had passed her discovery on to my mother, I secretly much admired her initiative.

Somehow I just knew that my great remedy would just have to be coloured purple, therefore an added complication clouded the issue. Everything that produced this essential colour was added to my potions. Blackberries were crushed into salt and vinegar, with sugar added just to balance the flavour, blue and pink bath salts were added to milk, bluebell flowers were pulped into rosehip syrup.

Some of the neighbours lilac was stolen but later confiscated by my mother who, on seeing me enter the house with it, proclaimed it unlucky. In fact, it proved only unlucky for me, for in my belief a vital opportunity and one holding much promise was being denied me. Despite all the setbacks and repeated failures of experiment after experiment I continued with my endeavours.

Then, one day, the experimenting was brought to an abrupt halt. Earlier I had heard about just such a fantastic magical ingredient, one that I had so far searched for in vain. A friend told me that his mother possessed a packet of crystals which turned everything purple. He said that he could steal them and would exchange them for my marbles. The deal was struck with mutual enthusiasm, and the contract was eventually fulfilled. I was overjoyed, beyond my wildest hopes, to find that these crystals, and just as I had been told they would, readily mixed with ordinary tap water to produce copious quantities of stunningly beautiful purple liquid. Surely I was now hot on the trail, only the finishing touches to my endeavours needed to fall into place.

Unfortunately, some of my precious crystals were lost in one experiment when I tried mixing them with glycerine, only to discover that the mixture spontaneously burst into purple flames. The fact that when mixed with water the liquid turned my hands brown was dismissed by me as only a

4

trifling side effect, and one to be ignored. To my unimaginative parents however, the fact that the crystals also turned the washbasin brown was definitely not to be considered trifling, or to be ignored.

An impromptu and heavily biased family court of enquiry was instantly convened. The upshot of which was that I suffered the rough justice of having to reveal the entire contents of my bedroom cupboard laboratory. There was to be no appeal against confiscation, and no mitigating circumstances were to be taken into consideration.

It was now the turn of my mother to be alarmed by the array of test tubes, bottles, pillboxes, tins and jars that came to light one after the other. Great alarm was to be unjustifiably expressed by both parents with the discovery that, among my collection of ingredients yet to be experimented with, was a small jar of deadly nightshade berries. Looking back, and since I had been the only willing guinea pig readily available, it is a wonder that I hadn't fatally poisoned myself. Fortunately, the only health cost to me was to feel slightly ill from time to time, and occasionally to be violently sick.

With my entire laboratory lost, and me now subject to oppressive security checks, pocket money stopped and the purchasing power of my marbles gone, I had only the laboratory of my mind left. Night after night nothing more dominated my thoughts than that elusive magical elixir. Even in my dreams I sought to solve the problem. Sometimes I did, only annoyingly to awaken having already forgotten the formula. Eventually both dreams and hopes were to fade, and somehow my mother miraculously survived.

Reluctantly I realised that the search had to be abandoned and the project, with all its investments, had to be written off. Fortunately the transition was eased by a compensating enthusiasm that was developing in my friend Charlie Price and me, to build our very own aircraft from orange boxes. However, my earlier dream was never to leave me entirely. One day in 1985, nearly forty years later, I finally discover a real elixir. It wasn't purple or even a liquid, instead it came in the form of black letters on white paper.

In short it was a correspondence course on hypnotherapy. This new found 'elixir' couldn't cure everything and everyone, but I quickly discovered that it did have an enormous potential, which quickly became realised as I went on course after training course, and put the knowledge and instructions that I gained into practice. My forty-year-old dream had finally become all but realised. Since that time thousands of people have benefited from that knowledge and the enthusiasm for healing that was born in me in those far off earlier days.

It is with enormous joy and satisfaction that, in the pages that are to come, I have attempted to hand over to the reader what I have come to know of the subject. Realising that in doing so, countless others will benefit from the experience of seemingly 'magical' healing.

Footnote: Should the reader wish to take up where my own experimentation was abruptly halted, the magical crystals, that seemed so near to bringing success, are still readily available today, and cost but little. Just ask your chemist for a small tub of potassium permanganate.

However, he will expect money for them, not marbles. However, the compensating benefit for this financial arrangement is that the crystals can be assumed not to have been stolen, avoiding the risk of being faced with the embarrassing prospect of being frog-marched up Aylesbury Street to confront David's angry mother. I have also since discovered they can do wonders in healing foot conditions, albeit in doing so, turn both bowl and feet brown too!

PART ONE

UNDERSTANDING
THE MIND'S ROLE IN HEALING

THE HUMAN ANIMAL

In animals, and we humans are of course a species of animal, the size of the brain relative to that of the body is an accepted indication of the animals progress on the evolutionary scale. We humans have by far the largest brain of all animals, relative to our body size.

What an amazing fact then, that the earliest signs of human activity ever found, are footprints that were laid down only three-and-a-half million years ago! On one now remote and distant day, a man, woman and a child walked across a volcanic ash covered plain, in what is now known as the Serangetty Park in East Africa. Following their passage the volcanic ash fossilised and preserved those foot prints, which can still be seen today. In a land teeming with wild carnivorous animals, and with only stones and simple spears to protect them, the footprints show that they walked with confidence, neither hurrying nor hesitating to check their security as they went.

Some quarter of a million miles from earth, across an airless void is the moon, and on that planet too are the footprints of mankind. An astonishing progress when compared to other life forms, many of which have only changed or advanced in their evolution but little in their of millions of years of existence. The common wood lice, for instance, has barely changed a hair in some six hundred million years. So how can it be, that in such a short geological time span, that we have become the most numerous and successful life form ever to evolve on earth?

The answer is not that we walked upright, leaving our hands free to develop our dexterity, but because we developed our intelligence! This not only gave us a unique and unchallengable advantage in the animal kingdom, but was to set us on the path to where we are today, and where we shall be in the thousands and even millions of years ahead. For our great adventure, on the time scale of planet earth, has only just begun.

That we humans should have even survived at all is surprising. In our earliest times we were surrounded by a host of predators, we couldn't run far or fast, we were muscularly weaker than them, we couldn't fly and neither did we have their thick skins, horny armour nor poisonous fangs to protect ourselves with. As if all this vulnerability were not enough we were, and still are, about the tastiest animal of all to carnivores and even to ourselves, hence the protracted continuance of cannibalism and even the success of Sweeney Todd's pies.

We survived, not just because of our dexterity but for another marvellous reason. We were blessed with intelligence. For most of our history we remained simple hunter gatherers but, with our intelligence to help us to survive, we grew steadily more numerous. All human life probably originated in Africa, 'the garden of Eden'. But then, with the combination of our adventurous inquisitive spirit and growing numbers, we began to slowly expand evermore widely over the globe, perhaps assisted by ice ages which dried up shallow seas and enabling our distance ancestors to cross them.

At first only the warmer lands became occupied, with the Indian Continent perhaps becoming a second 'Garden of Eden'. As our numbers continued to grow, less hospitable lands had to become inhabited thus creating a need for farming methods to be developed to bolster food supplies that were less naturally available. Gradually competition for land and resources evolved, leading to tribal warfare. Very slowly it became increasingly essential to make the most of what we had, particularly the more northerly we settled.

Humans are thought to have first inhabited the British Isles, a hundred-thousand years ago and probably only in the last few thousand years did the need begin to invent and make things. Once this process began, it to slowly started to evolve, with each invention and discovery making the next more likely. Over the last few hundred years the pace of discovery and invention, together with the ever increasing innovation, began to increase faster.

During this entire process of emerging technology, everything that has been required to satisfy the needs of advancement has been discovered, as if it had simply been waiting for us to want it. For example, coal came into it's own just as the Industrial Revolution needed it, followed by electricity, oil and nuclear energy. All the minerals and resources seemed to be there in the quantities we required, and at the time we needed them, and because of this the sciences have to continued to evolve, technology has improved and our knowledge has expanded. Now we have moved on from the Industrial Revolution and entered the first tentative years of the Space Age.

As part of this long history of progress, slowly and mostly little realised, there is another aspect of advancement. The understanding of the MIND itself, the very part of us that leads us to where we are and made us what we are.

Now, with countless millions suffering illnesses and diseases which conventional medicine can often do little to cure, a new realisation is dawning. That with our intelligence and the understanding of the mind we can inspire it to fill the gap in medical knowledge and heal ourselves of many of these conditions. This advancement too, seems to have arrived at just at a time it has become most needed.

THE HUMAN MIND

The human brain and how it works and functions has fascinated philosophers and scientists for thousands of years. Probably no one knows how many books have been written, how many theories have been put forward or how many ideas have been discarded in the process. In the early times it was the great philosophers who took the lead, gradually science and psychology began to take leading roles in seeking to unravel the wonders of the human brain. Fortunately for us we can spare ourselves from studying all the results of such a vast inquiry, and consider the mind, as the programme within the brain, in a simple and straightforward way. This is all we shall need to successfully conduct the 'magical' healing to be found in the pages to come.

THE FUNCTIONING OF THE CONSCIOUS MIND

The brain consists of billions of cells called neurons, and dotted throughout the brain are 'galaxies' of these that serve us as our intelligent brain parts. Each is linked to one of our senses, sight/see, sound/hear, touch/feel, taste/savour, scent/smell. These parts are in turn inter-linked with each other, and react with emotion to the occasion being experienced. Together these areas of intelligence constitute our conscious mind.

It is the task of our conscious mind to constantly analyse all that goes on around us. It constantly checks every input received by any of our senses, evaluating that information and deciding on the validity and importance of it and responding to it with any activity considered to be called for.

Surprisingly, at first, the conscious mind has no memory, is very slow when compared to the subconscious mind, and can only consider or think of one thought or matter at a time. The conscious mind constantly 'chats' to us, which is part of it's analysing and reasoning functions. Additionally, the conscious mind is happy to abandon it's responsibilities when we sleep, become unconscious or simply drift into an automatic mode. In this latter state we can drive our cars for miles barely being aware of the details. The conscious mind can drift into daydreaming, or become unaware of our reactions during monotonous routines or repetitive activity.

Despite all it's limitations and the seemingly part-time role it plays in our lives, the intelligent conscious mind is our greatest single asset, and is the part of us that has led us to our dominating position on earth.

THE FUNCTIONING OF THE SUBCONSCIOUS MIND

When the subconscious mind is examined we find ourselves confronted by an even more extraordinary mechanism. Estimated to constitute ninety-five per cent of the brain, the subconscious can be considered as being divided into two parts. The intermediate subconscious and the base subconscious.

The intermediate subconscious is fully attentive whilst the conscious mind is awake and active, going on 'standby' during sleep, when we see it's method of functioning in dreams. The base subconscious works twenty-four hours a day, neither sleeping nor resting. It is the task of the intermediate subconscious to be the 'go-between' of the conscious and base subconscious mind parts. That is, to liaise between the two.

The intermediate subconscious can be likened to some warehouse, containing the memories and emotions stemming from every experience we have ever encountered. The intermediate subconscious uses those memories it considers relevant to the current experiences and decision making processes of the conscious mind. The intermediate subconscious has a perfect memory, and it can perform many thousands of functions simultaneously. Between them the two subconscious mind parts also run and maintain our body for us.

The intermediate subconscious mind is very fast when compared to the reactions of the conscious mind. However, as will be stressed, the subconscious mind has virtually no intelligence, relying upon the intelligence of the conscious mind for that contribution, and combines this with the cleverness of the intermediate subconscious mind.

INTELLIGENCE AND CLEVERNESS

It is essential that the difference between intelligence and cleverness is fully understood, for this plays a vital part in understanding how the healing to be described actually takes place.

The intelligent conscious mind has the ability to encounter original experiences and situations, and to be able to respond to them with intelligence. To assess them and make original decisions, even where no similar experience has previously been encountered. It evaluates the environment and calculates responses and their consequences. This part of our mind is creative, imaginative, problem solving and intellectually talented.

The intermediate subconscious mind is extraordinarily clever, relying upon a perfect memory of all that has previously transpired to assist us with our thinking and decision making processes. As the intellectual conscious mind goes about it's analysing activities, it will be helped and assisted in it's reasoning by the intermediate subconscious mind, using it's vast store of knowledge.

When the intermediate subconscious mind feels that a strong enough reason exists to counter a decision of the conscious mind, then it will seek, and will often succeed, to cause the reaction it feels most appropriate. It is this which causes our reactions in phobias, panic attacks, unwanted habits, fears, the loss of confidence and the like. In short, intelligence is to do with the new, the original and creative, and cleverness is to do with the experienced, the known and previously learned.

The intermediate subconscious not only has virtually no intelligence, but is animalistic, caring neither for the right nor wrong, or the moral or immoral, leaving such considerations to the conscious mind, and the sense of standards and morals held by the intermediate subconscious given to it by the conscious mind.

In a simplified form, we can consider the conscious mind as our managing director who makes our decisions for us resulting from our current situation and needs. It is this part of the mind, as put forward previously, that first receives all the inputs through our senses, while we are awake and thinking rationally.

The intermediate subconscious can be thought of as our warehouse manager, retrieving stored information required by the conscious mind, that is, information previously passed to it by the conscious mind. In carrying out its functions the intermediate subconscious mind will do so relative to   previously stored information, and bring to the attention of the conscious mind any other linked factors stemming from past experiences and learning that it thinks relevant.

Using a similar comparison the base subconscious mind can be considered that part which repairs and maintains our bodies, co-ordinates physical reactions and fights infection. Collectively, given reasonable health and alertness, the system works brilliantly.

MIND FUNCTIONING EXAMPLES

Some examples of mind functioning may help to provide a simpler understanding.

Suppose you were told that two and two made five. This information would be received by your conscious hear/sound sense and be intellectually queried. "What? How come? "Why is this being said?" You might respond in some way but ultimately and probably quickly, dismiss the information as unacceptable.

Following the analysis of the conscious mind, this input, together with it's evaluation, would be passed to the intermediate subconscious. This would then be filed in the appropriate location within the intermediate sub-conscious or 'warehouse', as non-actionable information. Subsequently if someone else were to ask if anyone had told you that two and two made five, you would recall that they had, and in responding with 'yes', recall some of the emotion felt at the time of the original input.

If you were asked "How many legs does a dog have?" The question would again be received by your hear/sound sense and be queried there. However, the answer to the question is not a hear/sound one but a sight/see memory. Consequently the information must be retrieved from visually stored inputs.

Another way information is retrieved and acted upon can be illustrated using the following example.

You are asked if you would like some potato crisps. This enquiry is received by the sound/hear sense of the conscious mind, and aided by the intermediate subconscious mind the invitation will be considered jointly, causing a response by them. The response will be relevant to whether you are hungry or not, like them or not, and your environmental situation.

For instance, declining them whilst riding on the pillion seat of a motor cycle at sixty miles an hour would be predictable, whilst at some social occasion you were enjoying they would be more appropriate. Given that your response is 'yes please', the second sense to come into action is the sight/see sense. They must look right on being offered, green ones are to be questioned or rejected.

The next sense to become active is the feel/touch sense as the proffered crisps are taken up, soft or soggy ones are to be rejected. All being well the next sense to analyse them is the smell/scent sense, again they are to be rejected and queried if they smell of, say, pineapple. All being well so far, the last sense coming into play is the taste/flavour sense, should they taste bitter they will be rejected. Where the crisps are accepted and eaten the base subconscious will then take over, digesting and processing them, providing the acids to do so, extracting nutrition from them and finally rejecting the unused remnants.

In all of these reactions all three parts of the mind will participate, and in so doing will act as our safeguard with little or no conscious effort.

SUBCONSCIOUS MIND REACTIONS

Where no conflicting information is contained within the intermediate subconscious, the instructions and decisions made by the conscious mind will be responded to by the collective subconscious minds without question, and be reacted to instantly and automatically. For instance, when we consciously decide it is an appropriate time to cross a road, we will then instantly move forward in the direction and at the speed decided upon, with that decision only being countermanded should some change in circumstances be experienced - the sudden and unexpected approach of a vehicle for example.

Whilst all this is going on of course, the base subconscious mind is simultaneously maintaining and running the body as a whole.

Sometimes however, and in one way or another this otherwise brilliant system will fail us, breakdown, be bypassed, or simply become over-loaded, and it is for these reasons that it is necessary for us to understand the normal processes at work, and in order that we may correct them when they do fail or need assistance.

A SECOND MODEL OF THE MIND

It may help clear our thinking and understanding of the mind by using a simple model of it. In this model we have the intelligent conscious mind, the Managing Director, in the front office, receiving all the information from the environment, processing it and as if 'phoning' or 'posting' the conclusions and instructions to the intermediate mind. In the larger area standing the other side of a counter, we have the intermediate sub conscious responding in accordance with the vast store of information in the warehouse in which he stands.

Further back we have the 'machinery' of the base subconscious which the intermediate subconscious mind can adjust, and which maintains the body and causes both physical reactions and, where 'appropriate', bodily and physical malfunctions. A barrier over the counter could represent the normal difficulty of freely contacting the intermediate subconscious in the way we shall need to.

With the relaxation methods to be set out shortly, it can be imagined as if this barrier is raised, with the healing assistant joining with the conscious mind to work together, but in a more direct way of doing so. It is this arrangement which produces such effective healing results.

NEGATIVE EFFECTS OF MIND MALFUNCTIONING

Negative mind results can arise from many causes, and for practical reasons only some illustrations can be given.

The most common cause is the conscious mind failing to intellectualise an experience fully, and by doing so disrupting the collective subconscious. For example, when an experience is so impactive or sufficiently emotive that it becomes impossible for the conscious mind to properly evaluate the incoming information, either partially or wholly. When this happens, the collective subconscious will nevertheless accept the information it receives from the conscious mind from the experience as if it were factual and correct.

As an example, a young child is knocked over by a wave while paddling in the sea, and feels terrified as he struggles to stand up and run for the shore. Given sufficient mental anxiety at the time, the child might then increasingly shun, not only the sea, but other water experiences too, such as swimming pools, and go on to develop aqua-phobia - the fear of water. All this because the subconscious has been passed the information that water represents an unacceptable danger.

A very common form of mental disruption is one that can be termed faulty programming. In this the conscious mind accepts some information as factual and passes it to the intermediate subconscious in the form received.

This can occur even where little or no emotion is involved, with the inspiration for it's acceptance being the authoritative manner in which it is passed. This is the method used by the stage hypnotist, where the participants expect themselves to respond to the hypnotist and normally do so, rather as if a self-fulfilling prophesy.

Another, and even more common form of faulty programming, occurs when we are very young, and are more greatly influenced by our parents, teachers and peers. Not that such programming is all bad, but rather at that age we are more susceptible to accepting that which is faulty. For instance, we may be repeatedly told not to leave food on our plates, and then grow up and continue to feel guilty if we do, even as adults. The idea that if our parents were to cook a little less food, or match our requirements more accurately, a true saving of waste, may never have occurred to them or us. This form of programming often lies at the heart of our choices, preferences, convictions and prejudices.

A third way that our mental reactions can be adversely affected occurs in what might be termed the 'internal event repressed', and which usually occurs during sleep or unconsciousness. In this the intermediate subconscious 'reviews' some matter and comes to some erroneous conclusion, given sufficient alarm the intermediate subconscious will then proceed to conduct it's affairs as if that conclusion were factual, and to be incorporated into all further mental activities relative to that conclusion.

For example, generating nightmares, or the 'Oedipus Complex', in which the small boy can subconsciously conclude that the relationship between him and his mother is of an equal bond. That is, they are partners and that his father or brother is a threat to that relationship.

In the fourth form of mental disruption we have what can be termed the 'Negligent Factor'. It is this and the fifth form of mental disruption that mostly concerns us in these writings and our healing. In the Negligent Factor we find the base subconscious either over-looking some bodily maintenance task, or failing to realise that something is wrong with the body which requires attention.

It is easy, given the lack of intelligence at the subconscious level, where the responsibility for bodily maintenance exits, to understand how this can arise.

Firstly, just as the rest of the body and mind is human and not a machine, so too is the subconscious. Everyone has jobs and tasks that need attention. Some room that needs decorating, a lawn which needs mowing, a letter that should be written, or someone to be visited, any of which could be delayed or even never be finally concluded. In much the same way the base subconscious may fail in it's duties too! Hence, in many cases millions do suffer with arthritis and other bodily conditions.

In the healing methods to follow it is rather like encouraging someone to write that unwritten letter. Perhaps by saying, 'come on, lets do it now, I'll sit with you and help you, it will only take a few minutes, and you'll feel much better for it'.

In another way that the subconscious fails in it's maintenance duties, we have those, 'never thought about it' or the 'I didn't realise' reactions. In this case too the healing methods are just as effective.

In the fifth form of the base subconscious mind failing to maintain the body, we have the intermediate mind, concluding from the information it receives from the conscious mind, that the body should be allowed to deteriorate in some way, and then proceeding to instruct the base subconscious accordingly. Myalgic Encephalomyelitis, (M.E.) Multiple Sclerosis (M.S.) and Arthritis can all be typical of this reaction.

In the sixth form of bodily disruption we have the reflection of the high emotion of some experience being locked into or on the body. Period pains, eczema, psoriasis and an irritable bowel syndrome are examples.

PART TWO

HYPNOSIS - THE KEY TO THE SUBCONSCIOUS MIND

By now it is hoped that a good general understanding of mental processes has been put forward in an understandable way. However, to gain a good grasp of the subject, your patience in re-reading the texts, both covered so far and in the pages yet to come, will yield an abundant harvest of satisfaction when you come to put these writings into practice for yourself. Some may wonder how we succeed in surviving, given what has been written so far. Sadly too many have had to manage as best they can.

However, this should not be the case for the reader and his subjects, for you are acquiring the gift of Natural 'Magical' Healing, providing you with tools few others yet have, and with the knowledge you now have, we can proceed with our next step and begin to turn theory in to practice, and with all the satisfaction this promises, to spur us onward. For we need next to understand how to use our knowledge to bring about change, that is how to gain the co-operation of the collective subconscious mind to heal through relaxation - hypnosis.

THE INDUCTION OF HYPNOSIS

Self induction and the induction of others

For those who are not aware of having experienced hypnosis, a wide variety of opinions of it can be expected. Commonly those opinions will be wildly inaccurate. Among such opinions are that the hypnotised person is completely taken over by it; that no memory of the experience will exist; that hypnosis 'zonks' or 'zaps' the person out and that the person becomes some 'headless' victim of the hypnotic inducer.

Often, potential subjects will be much influenced in their thinking by the numerous portrayals of hypnotists as being 'spooky', 'evil', and having 'mystical powers' or 'dominating characters', each hypnotist eager for his next victim. The reality is that, apart from feeling more relaxed, no other sensation is felt! Consequently, at least at first the subject is in for a disappointment at how ordinary they feel. Often complaining that they are not in hypnosis, or erroneously deciding that it cannot be induced in them, and in this latter case, deciding it must be because their mind is too strong! Many people have watched hypnotists perform on stage or screen, and seen the hypnotised subjects carrying out actions or performing in a way that makes them appear to be taken over. These performances give a totally distorted picture of hypnosis. The stage hypnotist's subjects act in the way they do, and without realising it, because they both expect such reactions to occur and want them to. If they did not the hypnotist would be unable to make them do as they do. As an example of this concept consider the following.

THE FAILED EXPERIMENT

An American university's Department of Psychology reported that a professor had at first thought he disproved the theory that a person cannot be directed, in hypnosis, to act against their normal inclinations and behavioural patterns. Finding a female subject appearing to be highly responsive to hypnotic suggestion, it was suggested to her, in hypnosis, that upon de-induction she would immediately become physically aggressive to a selected fellow male student.

It was further suggested to her that when the professor clicked his fingers she would feel calm and stop the aggressive response. The experiment was successful and went according to the suggestions. The otherwise placid female, following de-induction and acting quite out of her normal character, had begun attacking her male student colleague. In repeated experiments the same female student was similarly induced to attack other students, which she subsequently also did. Finally, she was induced to attack her boyfriend with whom she was known to be deeply in love. Again a similar outcome was to result. Amazed at the success in overturning the previously held theory the professor, somewhat excited by his apparent discovery, thought to test his discovery further.

The following morning, amongst the much heightened enthusiasm of everyone, the professor once again induced hypnosis in the same highly responsive female student. He then proceeded to suggest that she again carried out an action, following the de-induction of hypnosis much in the same manner as he had previously suggested. This time however, instead of becoming aggressive it was suggested she would systematically undress.

Immediately the student abandoned the hypnotic trance, opened her eyes and smiled broadly. Somewhat taken aback, the professor asked her why she had reacted in such a way. Still smiling she replied "Well, I knew I'd be stopped with the aggression before any real harm was done in the earlier experiments, but this time I'm not so sure!" End of failed experiment.

18

ON REFERRING TO THE HYPNOTIC INDUCTION

By now it may have been noticed that when referring to a subject that has been hypnotised that I always refer to that person as in hypnosis, rather than under hypnosis. Although this is a personal point of difference in reference, I prefer it as in rather than under because, to me, under suggests connotations with other experiences, such a under the influence of alcohol, drugs and the like. So too the terms 'under the control of, under the thumb of, under a Court Order and under the conditions etc.! Each, to me, carries a negative implication, whereas, 'in control, in charge of, in the driving seat and in good health', carry positive implications.

A small point of difference perhaps, but think about it again and you may find the difference of implication important. A similar point of difference occurs with explanation to the subject of the hand passing induction technique to follow, where the subject is told that the healer is to bring his hand down towards his eyes not his face. For in a similar train of thought, many subjects will have experienced having been hit or smacked in their face, and may subconsciously react to the intended action with a memory of such an experience. In comparison, fewer would be likely to be reminded of any such experience by being told that, 'in a moment I will bring my hand down towards your eyes, and then I'll let it glide passed your nose, lips and chin'.

THE HYPNOTIC STATE

So what is hypnosis, or the hypnotic state? One might equally ask what is meditation in response, for hypnosis is similar to the meditation state. These are excellent examples of those simple questions that can be asked but be very difficult to answer. For even yet, what theories exist are subjective rather than objective.

However, hypnosis is understood in its principles. In the following I express my own personal interpretations. Hypnosis is natural and occurs frequently and spontaneously in all of us. 'Miles-away' daydreaming, watching television, listening to music and physically repetitive actions can produce it. Hypnosis is considered by many as a prerequisite state to enter sleep. In itself, hypnosis is entirely harmless, medically, physiologically and psychologically.

The hypnotised subject remains completely conscious in the hypnotic state, so too does the subject retain full control over himself, only acting in a way which is acceptable to him during the experience. The hypnotised subject will remember as much of what takes place after it as he would have in a non-hypnotic state. The subject can terminate hypnosis immediately and at his own behest, should he wish to - just as he might terminate daydreaming. The subject can also resist its induction if wished. Following the induction the only resultant feeling, if any, is of relaxation. We can now proceed with the methods of inducing hypnosis by turning first to considering the levels of hypnotic induction, the signs of it and the reactions of the subject.

THE LEVELS OF HYPNOSIS

Although the induction of hypnosis will vary from person to person, and of course from induction method to induction method, together with the various mind states during a given induction, broadly speaking four levels of hypnosis can be experienced. These are:

THE LIGHT TRANCE

As the first stage of hypnosis, this can usually be very quickly induced, and in even in less than one second. The hand passing method of induction is an example of this. In this the initial reaction of flickering eye lashes is very common, so too are the signs of changes in pallor, head drooping and appearing more relaxed.

THE HYPNOTIC TRANCE

Induced either by a psychotectic lamp or the other methods given, this is the hypnotic induction level most productive to the healing procedures given in this book. Any of the signs of hypnosis may occur, but often the subject will not be aware that hypnosis has been induced, where, paradoxically, those entering the light trance will be more commonly aware that some change has occurred.

THE SOMNAMBULISTIC TRANCE

Generally speaking the subject will seem sleep like in appearance, and as such may respond with slow slurred speech, or indeed be reluctant to talk. Most such subjects will be aware that they are in hypnosis and experience feeling extremely and beautifully relaxed.

Since the subject may enjoy feeling as he does, the healing may become less productive, with the subject less willing to be distracted from his sensations by co-operating with the healer. Such a situation can be likened to the one when we are sleepy and reluctant to talk to another. The induction of the somnambulistic trance normally requires an extended induction of hypnosis, perhaps best achieved through a combination of successive induction techniques.

THE CATATONIC TRANCE

This trance level is induced through an extended induction from the somnambulistic trance, and as such can require significant efforts on the part of the healer. In this the subject is so deeply relaxed that, just as if soundly asleep, virtually no responses may be given. It is this level of hypnoses that the 'entertainer' used to place someone with his head on one chair and his feet on another, and then have a third person sit on their unsupported stomach.

Indeed the subject is commonly rigid, but will allow movements to take place which are physically conducted by another. This is also the trance level that has been used in thousands of surgical operations without anaesthetics. During this trance the subject will not only feel physiologically numb, but feel no pain either. (Although the word pain itself should be avoided like the plague.) In this trance state, should a surgical operation be performed, two significant benefits are also experienced, a reduction of bleeding, and with a more rapid healing process to follow.

As an example of this trance level, I once witnessed such a subject sitting sideways on a chair, a volunteer offered to test the induction by pressing his knuckle into the subject's spine, and as hard as he could. Try as he might there was no further reaction from the subject than appearing to be pushed slightly forward. Exhausted by his repeated attempts the volunteer gave up.

Following the induction the subject reported only that he was aware that 'something' was happening behind him but didn't know what. When he was asked if what had happened hurt him then, or now, in some surprise he asked 'what do you mean?'

THE SIGNS OF HYPNOTIC INDUCTION

For those who use the psychotectic lamp to induce hypnosis, the signs that hypnosis has been successfully induced are more of interest in an academic way. However, of course they need to be known, if for no other reason than being able to demonstrate that hypnosis has been induced, say when a third person is accompanying the subject and it is considered beneficial for that third person to see the effect for themselves.

So too can it be beneficial to reassure a subject who has been de-inducted that the whites of his eyes that have turned pink is only a temporary effect, and a sign that hypnosis has been induced. However, having said all this, many healers, especially those new to inducing hypnosis, and those using less reliable methods, particularly those of an oral method calling for the subject to respond to his induction method, may feel a need to check the success of their induction. Probably the most common initial reaction from the subject, particularly with the hand passing technique, is the temporary flickering of his eye lashes.

In hypnosis some subjects will not shut their eyes completely, though they may be unaware of this. During this reaction they will be unable to see, since their eyeballs will have turned upwards.

Further indications of hypnosis are a noticeable change of facial pallor, involuntary facial expressions and bodily movements, and the drooping of the subjects head.

SUBJECTS REACTIONS TO HYPNOSIS

Most subjects have no previously known experience of hypnosis, I say they have no known experience because everyone constantly enters the state and almost never realise they have. 'Yes', they may agree, just as they are about to fall asleep that they have experienced odd ideas, pictures or thoughts in their minds. 'Yes', they will agree, that they have often driven for miles with their mind some place else. Probably everyone would agree that they have fantasised, and in some cases spending 'ages' in doing so. So too, many people will have 'dropped off' watching television, listening to the radio or music. Then their are those who meditate or have learned some successful method of relaxation.

All of these examples are forms and effects of hypnosis. Hypnosis is natural, commonly experienced and almost certainly essential for everyday life.

SELF-INDUCTION METHODS

There are many ways of inducing hypnosis. Follow your selected process and then carry out the work you intend. Don't be put off if you feel no different following the induction procedure, because using any of the methods given, at their conclusion, the hypnotic state will be present, even if it cannot be felt.

With practice, if not initially, sooner or later you will be able to detect its presence. In any case, it makes little difference whether you believe you have been successful in inducing it or not. Just try believing that the sun won't rise in the morning, and then check the sky the next day to see if it becomes light. As suggested, even if you don't feel any effect from the self induction, do the work you intended following the selected induction   routine. Sooner or later you will be in for a pleasant surprise with your results.

THE TEN TO ZERO TECHNIQUE

Lying comfortably in bed, first allow yourself the chance to relax. Then, with your eyes closed, choose an exhalation of breath and mentally label it as a number ten, doing your best to imagine a ten as you do so.

However, the lack of visualisation distracts little, should you find this aspect difficult, but it should at least be attempted. Perhaps you could visualise the numbers as if on doors, or numbers just floating weightlessly in the air, or some other personal mental visualisation will do. The better you have this visualisation the slightly more effective the induction is likely to be.

After visualising the ten, and on the next exhalation, repeat the method above but this time using the number nine. Now continue counting down in the same manner and to include zero. Following this begin counting again as before, but start counting from nine and go down to zero again. Following that, of course, count from eight to zero, seven to zero, and so on, ending with the final column of one to zero and lastly with a zero itself.

Repeat the entire exercise if you want to, but don't be surprised, if you do repeat it, to find yourself having drifted off into a pleasant sleep, with the intended work of course then left undone. Should you have the tendency to drop off to sleep during the first routine, then experiment with shortening it to leave yourself sufficiently awake to use the hypnotic state.

OTHER METHODS OF SELF-INDUCTION

THE GAZING TECHNIQUE

This technique for self-induction is better used sitting. Sitting comfortably, allow your gaze to fix on some object, say the small light reflecting and shining gently from some spot or surface - a flower, crystal or brass fitting, it doesn't matter what it is so long as it's not intrusive in its own right.

Gaze at it steadily, see details and properties in it that you may not previously have noticed. Think of its origins. If mineral, it had its origins in a supernova, the massive natural explosion of a star at least ten times the size of our sun. This rammed and fused elements one into another, and lit up our skies with a light greater than that from all the other stars of the night put together.

Somehow, through time, it has journeyed to become incorporated into planet earth, where it was eventually to be formed into its current shape. With all its properties it is now in your room, bathed in the light it now reflects, making it visible. Marvel at it, wonder at it. Its constituent parts are some fifteen billion years old. Now just gaze and think your thoughts of the great wonder to be found - even in something so small, or apparently insignificant.

Of course, you might just soak in the object's light or beauty. Whatever your thoughts, just gaze and become absorbed. After a minute or two, or when you just feel ready, say to yourself, (or think) "I'm going to close my eyes shortly, and when I do, I shall become deeply, deeply relaxed". Repeat this statement two or three times, then simply close your eyes gently. Continue to reflect on your chosen object for a minute or so, and then proceed with your intended hypnotic state task.

Note: Some people report that looking at a burning candle can produce excellent results. However, there is the question of safety to be considered should the subject then fall asleep.

THE HANDS DROPPING TECHNIQUE

Sit, placing the finger tips together, holding the hands around chin height and a little forward from your face, and momentarily gaze at them. Then, when ready, repeat three times: "I'm going into hypnosis", follow the third repetition by dropping your hands into your lap and closing your eyes as you do so.

THE ARM LOWERING TECHNIQUE

Sit, holding an arm out straight and above one leg. Gaze at a nail on one finger and keep gazing. As you gaze for about one minute, your arm will become heavier and begin slowly to lower. Try to make this lowering process as slow as possible. When the hand has reached, and is touching your knee, simply close your eyes.

THE MUSCLE CLENCHING AND RELAXING TECHNIQUE

Another method with wide acclaim is 'clenching and relaxing'. In this, with your eyes closed, you systematically tour the entire body including neck, shoulder, facial, chest and abdomen muscles, together with thigh, leg, foot, arm and hand muscles. Taking each part in a systematic order of your own determination, you first clench or tighten the muscle group, holding that tension momentarily while concentrating upon the part. Then relax that part while feeling the relaxation upon tension release. Again, the method can be repeated. The benefits of this method are both physical relaxation and induced self-hypnosis.

THE FIVE TO ZERO TECHNIQUE

The method lends itself well to such experiences of childbirth, dental treatments and similar situations that call for little intellectual contribution from the subject and where relaxation would help. It is also particularly useful in dealing with sudden shock.

For this method simply count down from five to zero while attempting to picture the numbers. Initially, the speed of counting may be as fast as is desired, but it should gradually be slowed if it is commenced at a fast rate. Eventually a rhythm should be aimed for where each number occurs on exhaling. The numbers are to be repeated over and over again; they, and nothing else are important. The numbers are to be forced into the conscious mind if necessary, and to become the dominant commanding point of attention. Everything else is secondary and inconsequential. This technique can quickly induce a state of relaxation and calmness.

DEEPENING SELF-INDUCTION

Whichever initial method you use, you can deepen it in the following way. Think to yourself, with your eyes remaining closed, "When I move my right hand I will be twice as relaxed again". Follow this statement with a small gentle nominal movement of the right hand. Pause, then following exactly the same procedure, continue with the right foot, to be followed by the left foot and left hand in sequence. As you proceed with these nominal movements and following the self-suggestive statement of "when I move my (bodily part) and saying (or thinking) I will be twice as relaxed again", the self induction becomes deepened progressively. This sequence can be repeated several more times.

The self-induction methods can of course be combined in ways of your own choosing. It is better to experiment to discover what suits you best. For those seeking to induce hypnosis without making any effort, simply watching a psychotetic strobe lamp for ten minutes is extremely effective, as well as being the easiest method of all. This should be done in a dimmed room to heighten its effect. There are excellent strobe lamps available which are especially made for this purpose. (The details of how to obtain one are given in the back of this book). These lamps are hugely successful in inducing a level of 'quality' hypnosis.

THE INDUCTION OF HYPNOSIS IN ANOTHER

THE EYE INDUCTION METHOD

Hypnosis can be induced by eye contact but this is a method I never use myself. Invite the subject to look into your eyes without blinking. You then appear to the subject to be looking back into his eyes without blinking yourself. Only the technique used is whilst appearing to look back into his eyes, your gaze is actually fixed on his forehead instead.

During this procedure suggest from time to time that he tries, implying the possibility that he may not be able, to resist blinking before you do. He then tries not to blink. If he fails, as he will do, you invite him to make a further attempt of beating you by being the last to blink. When, as is inevitable, he has blinked first after three or four attempts, reassuringly invite him to relax, close his eyes and keep them closed. Proceed if necessary to deepen the hypnotic induction you will have produced.

It is a variation of this induction method that gives rise to the saying: "Look into my eyes", that is so frequently heard of in connection with hypnotists. Since we are concerned with healing, such 'tricks' are not recommended, and the explanation of it is put forward more in an academic sense.

Other than the lamp and eye induction techniques, hypnosis can easily be induced in another by physical or oral means. Of course, you may also invite the subject to induce hypnosis in themselves, by using one or more of the self-induction techniques explained earlier.

THE HAND PASSING AND HAND SHAKING METHOD

In this method the healer is to make a small mark on the palm of his right hand, and then hold his hand about 40cm from the subject's eyes, with palm turned towards him and then say: "In a moment I shall bring my hand down towards your eyes, and as I do so, look at my hand using this mark (indicating the mark on the palm, with the left hand) as your focal point. When my hand is close to your eyes, it will glide down in front of your nose, lips and chin. When my hand glides down past your eyes just close your eyes and then keep them closed".

The statement is spoken softly and unhurriedly. Next, having carried out the action, say: "In a moment I shall pick up your right hand; don't help me at all, just let it remain floppy and loose". Then gently, while standing to the right of the subject, take his right hand and lift it about 25cm and gently rock it from side to side, say 15cm towards yourself, then back 30cm towards the subject - that is a 30cm arc swing is made.

As you conduct this gentle movement say softly: "In a moment, I shall count to three, and then drop your right hand into your lap, and when I do, you will be amazed at how much more relaxed you become. Here we go". Next count aloud to the rhythm of the three side-to-side hand movements - as described, and on the count of three, allow the hand to fall into the subject's lap. Move to the subject's left side, saying: "I'm coming round to take your left hand".

When on the subject's left, repeat the exercise as for the right hand. It is a good idea to repeat the entire exercise on a first occasion with a subject, because it is quite likely that the subject may have concentrated more on what you have been doing, than simply allowing the induction of hypnosis to happen. Moreover, once the subject is more relaxed about what is to take place to induce hypnosis, the subject will just let it happen. This induction is enough in itself for hypnosis to be sufficiently deep for work to commence. Flickering eye lashes and a slight change of the subjects posture or pallor are all good indications of a successful induction.

ORAL TECHNIQUES

In this method you merely talk your subject into hypnosis, and the following two examples will serve that purpose well. Please note however, no artificial voice projection should be used, just a gentle slowly paced, quiet presentation is best.

THE TRANQUILLITY INDUCTION TECHNIQUE

"(Name), please gently close your eyes and just let them stay closed. (Name), shortly, very shortly, you will begin to feel deeply and peacefully relaxed. And those feelings of relaxation are already beginning, and continue to bring an inner harmony to your mind. These feelings bring with them a sense of peace and tranquillity, so that you feel more and more relaxed. As you continue to relax, you feel good."

"As you become more and more at ease it doesn't matter if at times, you find your mind just wandering away to some pleasant thought, because your inner mind continues to listen and enjoys the growing sense of peace, harmony and tranquillity that is growing and developing within you now. (Name), you know those wonderful feelings that you can have when sleeping soundly, how you sometimes feel that you wish that you could just be left to doze and slumber. You remember how you felt, lazily laying on a lawn - or some beach in the sun, perhaps drifting in and out of a dozing sleep, yawning and just wanting to stay where you were."

"In a moment, I shall count slowly back from ten, and go all the way down to zero. As I do, you find that you relax more and more with each number I count, until, just as you've felt on those lazy occasions in the past, you feel deeply and beautifully relaxed once again. And as I count down I want you to feel yourself going down into calmness, peacefulness and tranquillity."

"Ten, feeling more peaceful. Nine, relaxing more and more. Eight, just keep gently listening to my voice. Seven, breathing more deeply and breathing more slowly. Six, becoming calmer and calmer. Five, becoming sleepier. Four, just lazily drifting. Three, becoming even more and more relaxed. Two, feeling as if you could just doze off into a deep and beautiful sleep. One, feeling calmer and calmer, more and more at peace. Zero, now totally relaxed, totally at peace, feeling tranquil and just resting."

"As you continue to listen to the sound of my voice, I want you to have a thought simply drift into your mind. Just picture yourself looking into a beautiful night's sky, and there, in the distance, seeing one solitary silver blue star, one solitary star, millions and millions of miles away. Just one tiny dot of light twinkling away. As you look at that star you are becoming ever more and more relaxed.

"You feel good, you are becoming ever more peaceful. As you do, just keep that tiny silver blue star as a picture in your mind, and soon, very very soon, you will find that you just drift off into a deep and beautifully feeling of peace and tranquillity. And as you do, I'm going to count down from ten, and go all the way down to zero again as you continue to relax even more and more."

"Just continue to listen to the sound of my voice, as you find yourself becoming sleepier and just drifting. From time-to-time you may find your-self almost dozing off to sleep, because you feel so peaceful, so at ease, so calm and relaxed, and each number I say is like a step deeper down into tranquillity, a step down into harmony and an inner peace."

"Now we begin. Ten, deeper down. Nine, just letting go. Eight, relaxing and feeling good. Seven, calmer and quieter, more and more peaceful. Six, deeper and deeper down into peacefulness. Five, feeling more silent and still inside. Four, feeling sleepy. Three, nearly all the way down now. Two, soon completely relaxed. One, down into total calmness and relaxation. Zero, now totally relaxed. (Name), there's no such thing as a hypnotised feeling, just a sensation of peace and harmony, and you are enjoying those good feelings now. Sometimes there are other pleasant feelings in hypnosis, some people feel a sensation of heaviness, or a lightness instead."

"These feelings may exist only in the arms or legs, but sometimes they may be felt all over, or change from one sensation to another. Sometimes a pleasant gentle tingling can be felt, but always there are feelings of harmony, relaxation, peace, tranquillity, and inner quietness, and you feel them now. Good feelings, wonderful feelings. (Name), shortly I'm going to help you, and as you relax even more and more, you find that your inner mind responds and participates in a fulfilling and satisfying way that delights you, as you begin to free yourself to become your true self - all feelings and ideas that you want to have, and grow to enjoy more and more."

Note: One problem which can occur with using oral induction techniques, is that the healer may not be aware of how the subject is reacting or responding to the induction. For instance the subject may have limited visualisation ability, or sometimes, may not find the method appealing enough.

Further to these points there is the question of speed of delivery, subjects vary in the timing they need to enjoy the maximum benefits from an oral induction. The following oral technique overcomes these problems, with the subject himself keeping the healer informed of his participation and response.

THE FLOATING TECHNIQUE

Note: To enhance the effect of the script to follow, its is best to proceed it with the hand shaking and hand passing method of induction, and follow this with the induction deepening counting technique to be given later.

Sitting at the subject's side, proceed softly and leisurely by saying:
"With your eyes remaining closed, I'd like you to begin to imagine yourself becoming lighter and lighter. Becoming lighter and lighter, until (pause) like a child's balloon at a fairground you can imagine yourself as if you are beginning slowly and gently to float up from the chair (pause) floating in the room. Say 'yes' when you are imagining yourself floating in the room". (await 'yes'). "Yes!"

"Now just keep feeling that lovely feeling, its just like the pictures you see of astronauts, floating weightlessly in space. Now, I want you to imagine yourself nearing the ceiling. (pause) Imagine putting your hand out to bounce gently off it, but finding that, without any sensation of contact, your arm just goes through it, followed by the rest of your body (pause) so that you find yourself weightless and in the room above. Say 'yes' when you are there." (pause) "Yes!"

"Now feel yourself weightlessly, effortlessly, floating on up until you float out of the building and out into the air outside. Say 'yes' when you are outside." (pause) "Yes!" "Now see yourself gently floating/moving away. Look at the scene below."

Note: At this juncture make some suggestions with a few seconds apart, of what they might see. Suggest as if they were taking snapshots of the things over which they pass, then keep helping with suggestions of town or countryside images.

Continue by saying: "I want you to keep going now, until you see in the distance the facade of a large stately home in the country. Say 'yes' when you see it." (pause) "Yes!" "Now float gently towards it, and when you arrive come down to land, very, very softly and gently, until you are standing on the large stone terrace in front of it. Say yes when you're standing on the terrace." (pause). "Yes!"

Continue: "In a moment, when I ask, I want you to feel yourself walking across that stone terrace, and down the five stone steps which lead down to the big beautiful green lawn - feel the sensations of walk-ing as you go. Now see yourself do that, and say yes when you are standing on the edge of the soft green lawn." (pause) "Yes!" "To your left is a beautifully carved stone vase full of beautiful flowers in perfect blossom and bloom. Just glance at it now and tell me what colour or colours do you most notice?" (pause for reply) "Now look to your right and tell me what colour or colours do you notice in the vase standing there?" (pause for reply) "Yes!"

THE INDUCTION OF HYPNOSIS USING A PSYCHOTECTIC LAMP

The major benefit of this method of induction is that a good quality of hypnotic induction can be relied upon, no effort is required by healer or subject, and the lamp can be used to induce hypnosis in another or one's self with equal effect. The lamp has a small red screen, which, when switched on, pulsates with a gentle on/off rhythm. This rhythm is fixed and therefore consistent. The viewer has merely to gaze at it for ten minutes, during which time he drifts into hypnosis. Following this induction, probably the easiest of all, the hand passing and hand shaking technique can be used with great effect.

THE COUNTING TECHNIQUE

Following the hand passing technique, a deepening of the hypnotic state can be obtained by using the counting technique.

Say to the subject: "In a moment, with your eyes remaining closed, I want you to count down from ten to zero, but in a rather special way. I want you to imagine each number in your mind before you say it out loud and then, between each number you first imagine and then say - and as if you can feel it happening as you say it, say more and more relaxed, okay? Do you understand what I want you to do?"

Explain again if the subject does not. Following his confirmation that he does understand, continue: "Okay, then call the numbers out". When the subject says 'zero', say to him: "Now, with your eyes remaining closed, bring that zero back on to the screen of your mind and hold it there. Say yes when you have". (pause). "Yes!" Continue: "Now I'll count to three, click my fingers and that zero will just disappear - watch it go. One, two, three, 'click'! Has it gone?" (pause) "Yes!" Repeat the counting to three and click your fingers again if the zero remains. This procedure, used with a subject already in an hypnotic state, can be expected to take him into the 'somnambulistic' level of hypnosis.

DE-INDUCTION

Following the induction of hypnosis, and any healing that has been carried out, de-induction is essential if the subject is then to return to normal activity. De-induction can be easily achieved by using the following script:

"In a moment, I'm going to ask you to return to the here and now, and then to open your eyes. When you do so, you continue to remain calm and beautifully relaxed, but be vigilant and alert, so that you can do what you need to do, like driving and walking, and all in the way you normally would. Now, when you are ready, come back to the here and now, and then when you have, open your eyes please.

Repeat the same message, should the subject be so enjoying the hypnotic experience that he is reluctant to come out of it.

In all my work, I have never experienced any difficulty or problem with de-induction - save for one occasion. In this instance a wealthy female subject refused my suggestion, reporting herself to be feeling too nice to accept it, and said she would happily pay the fees of my remaining subjects of the day to stay as she was, feeling so good. So much for the fears of those never having experienced hypnosis! Should you have induced hypnosis in yourself, a similar statement to the one given above, either thought or vocally expressed will happily serve the same purpose.

THE ADVANTAGES OF HYPNOSIS TO HEALING

As a professional healer I often explain the benefits of using hypnosis by illustrating a situation. "Suppose," I say, "that I bite my nails badly and habitually, a habit I couldn't control or stop, and I was invited to treat one hundred people with a similar habit. I would expect 95 of those I treated to stop biting their nails following a single session of therapy."

However, at the conclusion of the exercise one repeated a hundred times in all, I would still most likely remain a nail biter, because they would have received the therapy in hypnosis, but I would not have been in hypnosis.

It is interesting to speculate on how the mind has such very different capacities in hypnosis when compared to the non-hypnotic state. My own theory is that, and directly proportional to the degree that hypnosis exists in the subject, two main possibilities arise.

Firstly, (and there can be little doubt of this) the otherwise natural barrier between the subconscious and conscious mind is lowered or reduced.

Secondly, the mind's capacity to transmit and exchange memories, emotions, thoughts and reactions within itself is increased, either by reducing the electrical resistance to such transmissions, or because in hypnosis the mind experiences a heightened electrical discharge.

Of the two, I feel it more likely to be the heightened electrical discharge that creates the increase in mental transmissions and exchanges. Certainly the increase in electrical discharge could account for the commonly reported state of feeling 'washed-out' by subjects, following a particularly active session - the result, as it were, of using up resources to produce that electricity. A comparison might be made with a battery being subjected to a temporary heavy loading.

However, any washed-out feeling, unlike physical tiredness, normally soon recedes. Whatever does happen, hypnosis allows us, even more when worked on by another, to tap into that detailed memory of life and the vast natural healing capacity that we all have. Added to these possibilities is the fact that the more we deliberately experience the state the better the results tend to become. In the hypnotic state, we can even recall events occurring during sleep or unconsciousness. The following is an intriguing illustration of this principle, and of the limited intellectual resources of the subconscious.

THE CASE OF THE UNCONSCIOUS LADY

A young lady came to me, reporting that she not only had a phobia of roads which she could only cross if escorted, but had to walk on the path as far from the roadside as possible. Even then, she reported, she had to touch fixed objects like walls, railings and buildings as she proceeded. She was consciously aware of an experience she once had, and which she thought was the origin of her condition. She explained that when she was ten years old, she crossed a wide empty road with her grandmother, and in the middle of the road her grandmother had collapsed.

The girl shouted for help while remaining at her grandmother's side, but her calls went unheeded. With the stress of the situation mounting, she eventually collapsed, having fainted. (Fainting in this way, can be the illogical attempt by the subconscious to help the victim blot out an unacceptable emotional situation, so as to protect the conscious from further pain). The usual method of analysis was undertaken, and although it proceeded well, brought virtually no change of any significance.

Since she had previously recalled coming round quite soon after fainting, it had been easy during analysis, to make the mistake of thinking that the alarming incident itself was at the root of her problem, and that her abreaction of it would release her from her phobia in the usual way. However, this was not so - the conventional approach had failed and some-thing was missed.

Knowing that the subconscious continues to react and record, even during an unconscious state, I decided to explore the memories of that brief period of unconsciousness specifically. In the analysis, the subconscious did not make the deduction that any such information was connected with our quest. For my part, no indication was given that it was during the fainting condition that the phobia was laid down. In any case, such a situation is very rare. When her subconscious was specifically requested to reveal its thoughts after she had fainted, she spontaneously exclaimed: "Grandmother is dead and I shall be run over and be dead too".

The interpretation was: you can collapse on a road and die or be killed. Despite her grandmother surviving the incident, and the subject having no other negative road experiences, the self-programme had remained. The thoughts it produced were gradually reinforced, when subsequently crossing roads. Knowing of her subconscious thoughts, negotiation with her subconscious could succeed, which finally resolved her condition.

This last case has been included in this section on hypnosis, because it is an interesting example of the unusual, and because it illustrates how essential hypnosis is for resolving such cases. Without hypnosis I believe the resolution may never have occurred, and would have led to goodness knows what, for the lady was in a highly neurotic condition when she first attended for analysis, and only twenty one years old at that time.

PART THREE

AN INTRODUCTION TO HEALING

A NOTE ON THE HEALING METHODS TO COME

When reading the instructions for healing which are to follow, the reader could well be forgiven for finding them 'farcical', 'ridiculous' or as if some act of over imagination on behalf of the writer.

Some explanation is clearly called for. It is essential to remind ourselves that we shall be working through an intermediate subconscious mind that has little or no intelligence, but is very clever. This part of the mind converts all the information that it receives into pictures. Consequently it is infinitely better to 'talk' to it in a pictorial manner, and it is this factor which enables such rapid benefits to occur.

The pictorial healing ideas and suggestions given to the intermediate subconscious mind are instantly converted into instructions to be passed to the base subconscious where they are, in turn converted into an acceptable concept entirely compatible with natural ways of bodily healing and maintenance. The subject may be encouraged to imagine, for example, that he is troweling in a strong cement mix to some fragile or weakened bone. This will automatically be transformed to become a clear instruction for the base subconscious to strengthen the bone with natural bone material, not cement.

At first the instructions for healing may appear a little complicated. (Whereas, in practice, they are remarkable simple to use.) This is because, firstly, details have to be gone into in a way to equip the reader with variations of the procedures and to equip him for the various contingencies that may arise.

Secondly, the instructions may at first seem complex because describing even a simple activity, to someone new to it, and especially in the written form, can initially make that activity seem more complicated. Imagine, for instance, you had to describe, in the written form, how to go shopping, and to someone who lived in some remote land who had never seen shops as we know them.

With just a little confidence to try the methods, the reader will find them very easy and simple to use, and often taking only minutes to perform successfully. In fact, when I was filmed conducting these rapid natural healing methods for television, the crew repeatedly commented how amazingly quick and simple it all seemed. My response was "but what am I doing that anyone else couldn't do?"

'MIND OVER MATTER' SELF-HEALING

With an understanding of the mind, and knowing how to gain access to it through hypnosis, we can proceed with the healing techniques that can be used.

However, before commencing it is essential to emphasise that such healing should never be provided in lieu of medical attention, but rather as an addition to it, or to follow where conventional medicine seems not to be helping. It should never be suggested to anyone that they should either not consult a medical practitioner, or suggest he alter any prescription recommendations given to him by his doctor, rather that he should ensure that his doctor is kept fully informed.

'Mind over matter self-healing' is nothing new of course, but can often demand enormous willpower and take a lengthy time to bring effective results. Using hypnosis, in conjunction with the mind's natural imagination and imagery ways, the process of self-healing can be greatly speeded.

In what follows the healing is more concerned with the 'mechanics of the body' rather than with infection. However with infection, the method, may probably still be used, but in an attempt to strengthen the immune system.

Detailed medical knowledge and technical terms are neither essential nor even required by the subject. However, the healer himself should have at least a little more medical knowledge than the typical layman. Without that his ability to understand the nature of his subject's condition will be restricted, and his ability to assist may be limited to some extent.

Some basic knowledge of physiology is also helpful, and especially where it is up to the healer to describe to a subject, who cannot visualise the healing process for himself, how and what he is doing. When the healer is called upon to conduct the healing process he will need to ask the subject to follow his imagined actions, and this can hardly be done in the total physiological ignorance of the healer.

The most likely presenting conditions suitable for Mind Over Matter Self Healing are arthritis, bad backs, knee and neck conditions. However, as will be shown, many other conditions respond equally well. Subjects may also have a wide range of mysterious pains, aches and other conditions which have failed to respond to conventional medication, such as bones that fail to heal following a fracture, prolapsed introvertable discs (slipped disc), trapped nerves, arterial sclerosis and the like.

Since, in many cases, this healing need involve no touching, surgical operations, advice on life pattern changes, medication (by the healer) or diets, and instead only words and thoughts, it is probably one of the greatest discoveries for healing ever made. It is a wholly natural healing method, merely speeding up or triggering the bodies own healing process. Certainly, if all else has failed nothing is to be lost by the suffering subject in trying it.

In brief, Mind Over Matter Self Healing, in conjunction with hypnosis, is a very simple process of focusing the attention of the subject's intermediate subconscious mind on some affected bodily part. With the subject, in the simplest of terms and ways, then imagining recovery or repairs to be taking place. In our practice the technique is frequently used, and has been for years, and apart from a small percentage of failures, has never resulted in the slightest indication of any lasting negative effect.

Where the healing attempt fails to benefit of course, some other psychological cause may exist. Presented cases however are far more likely to be the result of some accidental neglect by the subjects' subconscious, of some part needing attention, than of a pure psychological origin. Since this method of healing is usually quick, as well as easy, it should normally be tried before psychological reasons for the condition are sought out.

The arthritic condition will serve as a good first illustration of the simple technique, particularly since this condition can mostly respond very effectively. Additionally, arthritis seldom, if ever, responds to conventional medications with a total permanent relief. Your subject of course, will know of this limitation of conventional medication.

37

The following case of a subject with an arthritic knee is used as an example of the procedure. The subject has agreed to attempt to rid himself of his arthritic knee condition, but doesn't believe it will work - non-belief is normal, but makes little if any difference at all, and this should be clearly pointed out to the subject before commencing. With the subject in hypnosis begin thus.

Healer. "(Subject's name), what I am going to ask you to do now is simply to imagine or fantasise that you are looking into that knee of yours, but from inside it, and at the part causing you discomfort. You may not have a photographic-like picture, but as you con centrate, an image will come into your mind. When you have that image or picture, just tell me what you are looking at".

Note: Await a response, and further encourage the subject, if an initial difficulty is encountered in visualising some picture or image. Perhaps by suggesting that they will shortly see some bone structure.

Subject: "I'm looking at some bone".

Healer: "Do you notice anything about it?"

Note: Be careful not to 'lead' as to what the subject might discover, unless difficulties are encountered by the subject in further visualisation.

Subject: "The bone looks dry, pitted and rough." (A condition commonly reported in arthritic conditions.)

Healer: "Good". "Now how could you fill that pitting?" (The subject, or failing that, the Healer may suggest some method.)

Subject: "I could fill it with the white filling that dentists use to fill front teeth".

Healer: "Good, tell me when you have done that." (The subject may take up to a minute to respond.)

Subject: "That's finished, I can imagine all the pits filled in now".

Healer: "Now how are you going to make the bone smooth?"

Subject: "I'll imagine myself sanding it down".

Healer: "Good, tell me when it's nice and smooth".

Subject: "That's it, it's nice and smooth, I'll just blow the dust off and it will be fine".

Healer: "Good, all the dust is taken away, tell me when you have finished".

Subject: "It's looking good now."

Healer: "Now for that dryness, should it be dry?" (If the subject says 'yes' it does no harm to continue as if he had said 'no'.)

Subject: "No".

Healer: "Then should there be some oil like substance coming from some where to lubricate it?"

Subject: "Yes".

Healer: "Then look for the end of the pipe that should supply it, and tell me when you have found it". (By now the subject has a good grasp of the technique, and is well on his way to success.)

Subject: "I can see it, it's like a garden hose-pipe, but there's not much oil coming out".

Healer: "Right, check if it's blocked, poke something inside it."

Subject: "I poked a small cane into it but it's not blocked".

Healer: "Then follow it back, see if it's twisted or trapped".

Subject: "No, it's fine".

Healer: "Then go back to the tap and turn it on more, until the oil flows freely".

Subject "It's coming out properly now, there were a few splutters as air pockets came out, but it's O.K. now." (In very rare cases, turning the tap on may still not produce the oil flow. Should this occur, suggest going back to the mains and turn that on. Going even further back through the mains system, if necessary.)

Healer: "Now look at that oil coming out and describe to me what's happening".

Subject: "It's running all over the bone".

Healer: "As you sit in the chair what does the knee feel like now?"

Subject: "It's warm, (pause) and it's tingling a bit, (pause) funny sort of feeling, but nice." (The sensations reported are confirmation of the healing taking place, however, about one subject in three will report no such feelings. The absence of such feelings does not normally mean the healing has failed.)

Healer: "Does anything else need attention in there?" (Normally the subject will say 'no' in a case that has proceeded as this one has, however, and to further illustrate the technique, the therapy could continue as follows.)

Subject: "Yes, the muscles seem a bit tight, and are a darker red than they should be".

Healer: "How could you loosen up those muscles?"

Subject: "I don't know."

Healer: "You know how some wives plump up cushions and pillows, do you think you could do that with those muscles?"

Subject: "Yes, I'm doing it now (pause) they are all beginning to look relaxed".

Healer: "Good, are they still a too darker red?"

Subject: "Yes, but not so bad now".

Healer: "What colour should they be to be right?"

Subject: "Pinkish".

Healer: "How are you going to turn them to that pinkish colour?"

Subject: "I'll just watch them turn pink (pause) and they are turning pink now".

Healer: "Good, tell me when it's all done?"

Subject: "They look good now".

In what has taken place, the intermediate subconscious mind has been focused upon a bodily part, in this case a knee, and has been induced to carry out natural healing. It doesn't matter what colours, conditions or parts are imagined, nor does it normally matter what remedies are applied - except with arthritis, where 'oiling' should always form an essential ingredient. This is because the mind understands and interprets them.

In short, the subconscious has now realised something to be wrong and rights it. By using similar methods a subject can deal with sprained muscles, tendons and torn ligaments etc. He may be invited to ensure all the bones are in their correct places and moving smoothly.

What has seemed as an act of over imagination turns from comical disbelief to amazement for Healer and subject alike, as the subject reports either some relief, a considerable improvement, or total recovery. In some few cases a second, or more rarely, a third attempt may be needed. The idea that such a process could do any harm stretches incredulity to its ultimate extreme. Only those who have never tried it, or observed the healing method are truly authorised, by their ignorance of it, to scoff or laugh.

The same fundamental principles apply with many conditions and a few examples of actual cases are to follow. Before proceeding however, it must be re-emphasised that the images and mental methods employed in this self-healing technique can verge on, or even seem, totally ludicrous. The mind itself will differentiate between those images and methods and what it really needs to do, and do none, some, or all of the healing.

Note too, that while the mind may over deliver, say excessive calcium deposits, such as in osteo-arthritis, the mind can also remove it. Though it will take repeated attempts and therefore longer to achieve change, pain relief is likely to be swifter. Where excessive deposits are set in progress of removal, no deterioration of the basic bone structure will be experienced.

In self-healing, the mind is bringing about change in accordance with the subject's original self-blueprint or genetic instructions. In any case, by way of a double precaution it would be enough to emphasise that the bone, or joint, is visualised looking healthy and strong as part of the imagery and suggestion process.

As in: "Now you see the excess calcium beginning to dissolve and going away, rather like snow melts and reveals the surface below. See how strong and healthy the natural bone structure is underneath, see only the excess is melting away, and leaving that strong clean healthy bone underneath, just as it should be, and just as it was designed to be. Tell me you can see it just like that".

THE CLIENT WHO VISITED BY MISTAKE

In one rather amusing case, as it transpired, a client rang to ask if we were "Any good with bad backs?" Saying that for eighteen months he had been off work, and was often in agony and unable to get out of bed. He added that his previous physiotherapy sessions had all come to nothing so he wanted to try private treatment. We agreed to see him, saying that we could guarantee nothing.

The man made his appointment and eventually arrived, walking with two sticks and assisted by his mother. Placed comfortably in an armchair he asked, with some intense curiosity, how his back was to be treated with him sitting as he was. When my wife explained the procedure he confessed to his mistake. In going through the yellow pages he had mistaken our entry as psychotherapist for physiotherapist.

However, following the explanation of the proposed treatment he decided, having made his journey, it was worth giving it a try. The healing proceeded roughly as follows:

Gail: "Now, what seems to be wrong down there?"

Client: "There's a bone out of its socket".

Gail: "How can you fix it?"

Client: "I'll put a rope around it, throw the other end over that rib, and pull the bone into line with its socket".

Gail: "Tell me when you have done that".

Client: "Yes, it's in line".

Gail: "Right, what do you need to do next?"

Client: "I'll bang it into the socket with the palm of my hand".

Note: Client lets out a squeal, but reassured my wife that he was all right.

Gail: "What do you need to do next?"

Client: "I think I'll knock a nail through the joint, and bend it over at the back so that the bone can't come out again".

Gail: "Tell me when you have done that?"

Client: "That looks fine, the joint can move easily, but won't come apart now".

Note: Further exploration revealed nothing else needing to be done. The client was to leave, both sticks carried in one hand, and to swivel at the waist as he waved good-bye. Several months later my wife met his mother in town. She reported her son had gone back to work, no longer had any pain, and was 'over the moon' with his treatment. Of course, no claim is made or suggested that a competent osteotherapist or physiotherapist could not have achieved the same result. The case is put forward as just a further example of what Mind Over Matter Self-Healing can achieve.

THE GIRL WHO AWOKE CRYING

In another case, a young girl reported internal pain attacks that were intense and came on during sleep, causing her to awake crying, and which lasted for hours when they occurred. All medical investigations had revealed nothing detectable to be wrong. She was treated as an emergency case, actually during an attack, at one o'clock in the morning. Despite her tears of pain, and only being nine years old at the time, with great courage and strength of character she quickly grasped what she had to do.

Following her mental inspection she reported that she could see a dark red area that should have been pink. Asked how she could change the colour, she responded by saying she could colour it in pink with a felt tip pen. This she was invited to see herself doing until it was completely coloured in pink. After a few moments she reported this done and there to be nothing further to do.

The pain rapidly subsided and in some ten years since no further attacks have occurred. The case is well known to us, since the girl is our own daughter. In the years preceeding her treatment, sadly we lacked the knowledge set out here, and we were the first-hand witnesses to her previous agony.

MY EARS HAVEN'T GROWN PROPERLY

In another case a young girl was brought to us suffering from an ear condition in which her ear had not properly enlarged as she grew. One conventional medical treatment method, is to insert a grommet into the ear to expand it. This is often a painful treatment, taking time to effect. The mother, knowing of us and our methods, brought her to us to explore the possibility of an alternative approach.

During the therapy, the following transpired. The girl was asked to imagine herself looking into her ear, and to say what she noticed. "It's too small", she responded. (In this obvious answer it didn't matter that it probably derived from her conscious expectation, because it was not only true but served to bring her subconscious to focus in on the part anyway.)

"How could you make it into the proper size?" "I don't know" she replied. "Then supposing it were made of something softer, something that you could enlarge, like plasticine, you could then see yourself gently running a finger or thumb around it, slowly making it larger couldn't you?" she was asked.

"Yes". "Then try that" she was invited. A few moments passed. "How's it going?" she was asked. "It's working! it's working!" "Good, just keep on until it's perfect". "I've done it! I've done it!" She reported enthusiastically. "How does your ear feel now?" "Warm". "Is the discomfort still there?" "No it's gone".

No further treatment has since been required. We know this because the mother is also a friend of ours. Many of those treated using this method are local people that we subsequently meet, and consequently, we are able to follow the progress of such clients. In no treatment have we come across a case of relapse or subsequent deterioration.

Furthermore, changes can be expected to be confirmed where a subsequent medical examination is conducted - such as x-rays. That is, the changes are not imaginary, or some symptom stifled by suggestion, but actual changes, and brought about by a seemingly unbelievably simple method! This healing technique offers humanity an enormous opportunity, one at least as great as the introduction of vaccinations or the discovery of penicillin.

IT'S O.K. I'VE ONLY SPRAINED MY WRIST

A further case illustrates the concept of the technique rather well. A middle-aged man reported that he had a very weak wrist, and that bones in it were easily broken. Nothing had been found to strengthen it and only this part of his body was affected in this way. As a matter of safety he had to wear a metal support, coated in pink plastic.

This was heavy and although used to it by then, it greatly restricted both the use of his wrist and hand. Since it was also his right hand, his problem was compounded. Following the induction of hypnosis and the usual way of instructing him in what he should do, he was invited to 'look' inside his wrist and report what he noticed about the bone structure:

Client: "It makes me feel sick to look at it, it's like crumbling chalk, and full of pits and holes - there are some lumps too".

Me. "What do you need to do first?"

Client. "Take a nail file and file off the lumps".

Me. "O.K. See yourself doing that, and tell me when you have finished".

Client. "It's filing off easily, (pause) - they have all gone already".

Me. "How are you going to fill the pits and holes?"

Client. "With a strong mix of white cement".

Me "Tell me when you have done that".

Client. "It's done - and getting hard fast".

Me. "O.K look around, and tell me if anything else needs doing?"

Client. "No, everything seems all right".

Note: A week later he had discarded his wrist guard, and reported himself to be using his arm and hand normally. The third week he came to me for his session of analysis with his arm in a sling. Seeing me look at him openly disappointed he smiled. "Don't worry," he said, "It's O.K. - I've only sprained my wrist". "I was so pleased with my progress that I decided to test it, in case I was just imagining it to be better" "I deliberately worked it hard, knocking my garden back into shape, and in doing so I sprained it." "But it didn't break!" The healing method was immediately used to ease the sprain, with him leaving with his sling in his pocket. The man's next x-ray, showed everything to be normal.

I frequently demonstrate this healing method during talks and lectures - including those given in hospitals, since it is the quickest way I have discovered of demonstrating what amazing benefits hypnosis can bring. Especially since instructing the subject in what to do, inducing hypnosis and carrying out the healing itself normally takes only some fifteen minutes in all.

When this time scale is compared to the many hours that can be spent in visiting specialists, a period of over three years in the case of the man just reported with the wrist problem, the effectiveness of the treatment speaks for itself. Especially in some accident recovery cases this reduced time factor can be even more dramatic.

You may wonder why this simple healing method is not better known. Well, apart from this being another of the main reasons for writing this Book, the problem is that we are once again back to that intangibility barrier. But even more so, because the method is so ludicrously simple that its very simplicity is its greatest barrier to credulity!

As a result people find it difficult to believe. Even the experienced Healer constantly finds it amazing. I still have that difficulty now, but to a much lesser extent, yet I have used it successfully many hundreds of times, and I have twice been shown demonstrating it on Television. During the filming the camera crews, programme producer, lighting and sound technicians all reportedly expressed their amazement at how simple I made it all appear, and all with subjects that I was meeting for the first time.

If this therapy came out of a bottle or arrived in tablet form, it would be hailed internationally as one of the greatest healing remedies ever to be discovered, and would be immensely profitable to the pharmaceutical industry. It would also be headline news, and become the subject of endless television and radio reports. Yet it is here now! In my numerous attempts to spread the message, I once wrote to a hundred and twenty doctors offering to demonstrate it free of charge. Frustratingly, only one replied, and he then later declined!

46

On one occasion, during a lecture to a club at which doctors were present, I asked if anyone had a problem that they thought might respond to the healing technique that I had just explained to them. A volunteer came forward and said that for years he had had a neck condition that made turning his head, with any more than a very limited movement, too painful to do. Everyone else present knew of his condition since it was conspicuously obvious from the way he had to turn his body to look left or right. With my 'fingers crossed', hoping that he would prove to be a co-operative subject and be able to play his part, I agreed to make the healing attempt.

Having explained what I wanted him to do, and hypnosis having been induced, the procedure was followed until the volunteer reported nothing further needed doing. Following the de-induction of hypnosis I was relieved to see him smile, and hear him say it felt much better. I next asked him to try turning his head. Continuing to smile he did so, reporting in some amazement that it was 'back to normal' and he began turning his head from side to side vigorously. There was a gasp from the audience, then some member sarcastically shouted out: "What's your name - God?" as I so often find myself thinking, ah well!

The overriding value of Mind Over Matter Self Healing is its simplicity. While hypnotherapy is destined to become one of the most, if not the most important part of mental health care in the future, this simple healing method is similarly destined to hold equally high office in physiological care.

When this therapy is the subject of a lecture, I often say to my audience: "If you want a good laugh listen to this, and if you want to be amazed witness it in action, preferably on yourself". A further valuable aspect of the method is that you can use it on yourself. But it is better if someone is with you, because that will help to keep you concentrating and working systematically, adding discipline to the procedure. Also, having someone with you will heighten the effect.

Some more illustrations are called for.

THE LADY WHO LOST HER BREATHING PROBLEM BUT DIDN'T KNOW IT

A lady attending for analysis reported that before each session could begin she would need a minute of two to recover her breath, since climbing my stairs left her panting and breathless. I asked her about her breathing problem, and she explained it had been caused by her smoking. She had quit smoking some years before but her breathing had never returned to normal, and her doctor had told her nothing could be done. When I explained the healing method she was highly sceptical, but agreed to try it. Using the standard introductory approach, I asked her which lung she wanted to work on first:

Client: "My right one, that's the worst, and sometimes I feel pain there, but nothing shows on the x-rays I have had".

Me: "Go into that lung and look around it. Tell me what you notice?"

Client.   "The walls of the lung look blackened, like smoke stains in a chimney".

Me.   "How are you going to clean it?"

Client.   "I'll spray it with a kitchen hand spray cleaner".

Me.   "Okay, Tell me how it goes?"

Client.   (smiling) "The stain is running off".

Me.   "Good, there is a drain there somewhere, can you see it?"

Client.   "Yes, it's like a road drain, and all that black stuff is running into it".

Me.   "Good, keep going until all the stain has gone completely, and tell me when it has."

Client.   "Yes, it looks lovely and clean, it's a bright pink now".

Me.   "Great. Is there anything else you need to do there?"

Client   "Yes, I think I will put an open Vick bottle on that shelf over there, to give me a boost".

Me.   "Good, tell me when you have done that".

Client.   "It's done. Everything looks good and I'm breathing more easily too".

She then followed the same procedure on her left lung. Attending her next session there was no hint of any breathing difficulties at all. When this was mentioned she responded that that must be because she had been walking much more, and the exercise, with the better weather, had made her fitter.

In fact, in a series of bad weather weeks, the preceding week had been even worse. When I asked her about how much extra walking she had done, and if it had made her breathless at least at first, it appeared that she had only done a little more walking than usual, and she said that she hadn't any experience of breathlessness.

She continued to the end of her last session to dismiss her change as having anything to do with the 'innocent fantasy exercise' we had conducted. This case illustrates another reason why this technique is not more widely known. She certainly would not tell her doctor or anyone else. For her, at heart, any connection between her improved breathing and the treatment was a myth. Ah well!

ROLLING ON

A friend brought her ten year old daughter to me saying that her daughter's ankle was so painful that she could only walk a few hundred yards. Her daughter had had extensive medical investigations but nothing wrong could be found. She said that her daughter was also upset by having to be excluded from games at school, and was far from enjoying life because of the near constant pain. During the healing procedure the daughter reported she could 'see' a nerve out of place, and stretched over the 'knob' of a bone.

She saw herself resolve this by applying some hand cream to make the nerve more supple, and then gently ease it into its correct position. That was all she reported needed doing. This was all years ago. Since then she has experienced no further pain, except for being badly bruised in a high speed accident when roller skating. A hobby she is much into these days and at the time of writing, is now aged eighteen.

'I CAN DO HAND WALKING AGAIN'

On another occasion a 16-year old girl reported that she would need time to climb the stairs to my office - they are only a normal domestic flight - because of her painful knees. I suggested Mind Over Matter Self-Healing be tried, but this offer was initially declined, since she was shortly to have an operation following a long time on a waiting list.

Prompted by the suggestion that she had nothing to lose, she eventually agreed to try. In hypnosis she reported that neither knee cap seemed to fit properly. Seeing each in turn rather like manhole covers, she smoothed the rims by imagining herself putting some grinding paste around the rim of each, and then using a bar with handles that locked into a slot in the top of the covers, saw herself rotate them until they ground themselves into a neat fit.

Following this, she imagined herself removing them and cleaning each before replacing them. She not only ran down my stairs at the end of the session to test them, but on returning told me that she could do hand-walking again. (Hand-walking requires a constant fine balancing action through both knees.) Although I declined to advise her on whether to proceed with her pending operation, telling her to discuss it with her doctor instead, she later told me she had decided to cancel her operation, seeing no point in it.

Although the healing technique in itself is not painful, the changes brought about by using the process can cause some discomfort to be felt, because of the actual physiological changes resulting from it. To put this into perspective, the worst experience of discomfort that I have witnessed came in the following case:

THE LADY WHO WAS DRIVING
HER FAMILY UP THE WALL

The attending lady was then aged eighty-six, mentally alert but highly neurotic. Her exasperated family brought her to me saying she had reduced them all to nervous wrecks and, what was even worse for them, she couldn't go out without at least two family members in attendance, because she often fell over.

Between the three family members, who had brought her the thirty miles from where they lived, they got her into my office and practically threw the lady into my chair. The lady could see I was cross at her treatment but said it was all right because she knew she was driving them all up the wall and deserved all she got. On fetching her the glass of water she requested, I saw my dining room in which the other three sat, blue with smoke as each chain smoked away their nerves grumbling about her.

I suggested to the client that it might be a good idea to begin our work by trying the healing on her legs, in which she reported having little or no sensation. She readily agreed. As I sat beside her we began to work on her right leg. She took to the method like a duck to water. It quickly became a matter of me just sitting with her while she reported a constant stream of corrections and changes to nerves, joints, muscles, veins and tendons.

This all took much longer than would normally be expected, and was taking up more time from the hypnotherapy session than I wanted, but what was far worse the lady began to report increasing pain as she worked. Eventually the pain grew to such an extent I became alarmed, and suggested the attempt should be interrupted. Despite her obvious pain she insisted on continuing. I expected her cries to bring her family bursting into the room at any moment - she had been brought for me to help her, and I had apparently reduced her to agony instead.

Fortunately the pain eventually began to subside, and when it had done so enough I took my leave to go and reassure her family, who, much to my relief, showed only minor concern, and were all still smoking away. Somewhat relieved I returned to my office, and was aghast on entering, for I found the lady once again in considerable pain, with tears not wiped away and rolling down her cheeks. She opened her eyes, and briefly smiling said, "It's O.K., I'm working on the left leg now."

The session lasted ninety minutes in all. I wasn't surprised to find my next client, waiting his turn pacing the garden. There were nineteen cigarette stubs in the ash trays when they left - still smoking. Over the next three weeks her legs were to return to normal, allowing her to get out of the house on her own. This, with the gradual process of relieving her of her neurosis, brought a whole new harmony to the household.

MIND OVER MATTER SELF-HEALING
FOR ANOTHER

In this, rather than guiding a person through the healing procedure, the Healer himself imagines doing the work for the subject. Some explanation is called for. Say the subject reports that he cannot imagine the affected part, is too young to understand, or even in a coma. In such circumstances, it could well be worth the Healer taking on the healing task.

Sitting beside the hypnotised subject, begin by closing your own eyes to aid concentration, and then vocalise your own mental pictures. Much as if, with your knowledge, you were healing yourself. However, the subject is to be encouraged where possible, to imagine as best he can what is being explained, and to take part in a vocal exchange as the healing proceeds.

As an example, I quote the following case. A client reported that she had a 'floater' in her right eye, and said it had been diagnosed as a bag of trapped fluid. She said the floater gave her a similar visual effect that one wearing glasses might have, from having a small rain drop in the centre of one lens that could not be wiped off. It was a very uncomfortable condition, and one that had persisted for years. Since it was her eye itself that was affected she found it impossible to imagine herself 'seeing' into it, and asked that I should conduct the treatment. In hypnosis the healing went as follows.

Me.   "I want you to imagine that I have a microscopic vacuum tube that it is very, very thin. Shortly, I shall carefully and gently move this forward between the fibres of your right eye, and towards that floater. Tell me when you can imagine that tiny vacuum tube."

Client. "Yes, I can picture that."

Me.   "Now I'm gently moving it forward, slipping it easily between the fibres. Tell me if you can imagine that?"

Client. "No, not really."

Me.   "O.K., It's going forward nicely, and I am very near to the pocket of fluid. Shortly I shall reach it, when I have I will tell you. Then I shall ask you when you are ready for me to push the microtube into the floater (pause) - I am there now. Say 'yes' when you are ready."

Client. (after a slight pause) "Yes - ready."

Me.   "It's gone in, did you feel it?"

Client. "Yes, I think I did."

Me.   "I'm switching on the vacuum now, and the fluid is draining away very nicely, can you imagine that happening?"

Client. "Yes, yes."

Me.   "It's nearly all gone now. (pause) - there, it's empty. Can you picture that?"

Client. "I'm not sure, my eye feels different, but I can't explain how."

Me.   "Good, now I'm going to move forward, until the vacuum tube touches the other side of the bag." "When I do that, the bag itself will be drawn into the vacuum tube, leaving the eye perfectly normal." "Say yes, when you are ready!"

Client. "Yes."

Just before leaving the lady reported that she could still see the floater, but it was so small she had to look for it. Since I have not seen her since, the outcome must be considered inconclusive, but it does illustrate the method in use.

HAND-HEALING

Broadly speaking this method would be better understood or imagined by likening it to faith healing. The hands are to be used to conduct the process. The hands should be placed over some affected area or contacting it.

THE METHOD ILLUSTRATED
(Without Physical Contact)

A subject reports a painful neck condition. With the subject sitting, the Healer holds one of his hands, palm turned towards the subject's neck, and a little away from it. In a like manner, the Healer places his other hand over the subjects head. By gliding his hand up and down the neck slowly, while moving his other hand over different areas of the subject's head, including, and in particular, the forehead, normally a distinctly cool area in the neck area will be detected. Mostly, in less than a minute, the subject will smile, and report a tingling sensation, and then that the pain or tension is lifting. Once this has been reported, the healing process will continue, even if the Healer should stop his action at that point.

Exactly the same procedure can be adopted with the common headache. In this, both hands are used over the head, searching for hot or cold spots, or being guided to the pain area by the subject. This procedure can be conducted without hypnosis, and can be done by anyone. The total time taken is around fifteen to thirty seconds in all. I have found no quicker way of impressing someone, and therefore gaining their rapidly increased confidence in me, or capturing the attention of my audience at a lecture, where a suitable volunteer comes forward, than demonstrating this simple technique. You must try it, even on yourself to believe it.

This technique was described, and successfully demonstrated, to a lady subject attending a session and reporting that she had a headache. Late in the evening, and rather tiddly, she rang from a noisy pub and excitedly reported that she had just cured her friends headache, apologised for ringing so late, and hung up.

(Despite its simplicity though, I must temper enthusiasm with caution. Several husbands have reported total failure in their attempts to use it to help cure the headaches of their wives, which from time to time mysteriously occurred on going to bed. However, such set-backs should not stop you trying.)

On one occasion I demonstrated this headache 'lifting' method on the radio. It was a chat show, with myself and three other Healers from different disciplines. On arrival, and before we went on the air, the host said how he had already had a long busy morning, and hoped the show would run smoothly because he had a bad headache. He had a special pill for his type of headache, but added that he tried to do without the pills when possible. I immediately asked a female guest to carry out the headache lifting procedure, which she did. Neither host nor fellow guest having the slightest previous knowledge of it, both were jointly amazed at the rapid effect that took place.

At the end of the show, and over the air, (I still have a recording of the event) the host confessed, although he didn't like to, that he had had a headache before coming on the air. He then described what had been done, and he continued by saying, "I'm a cynical old-so-and-so as I'm getting older you know, and I was determined this [headache lifting] wasn't going to work. And that I was going to be able to say it didn't do anything for me. I even brought a headache tablet with me, because I felt it was going to be a bit of a stinker of a headache, [and] I haven't had to use it yet. Well, it's certainly been an eye opener." The others however, were to dismiss it as some inexplicable coincidence or sharp-practice, brought about by some concealed suggestion. I was quite disappointed with their reaction.

THE HEALING IN PRACTICE

In the previous text Mind Over Matter Self-Healing was put forward in a more 'general' context. From this point onward conditions are to be gone into more specifically.

As you will see from the text, most conditions are first described to help the Healer understand them, the suggested healing method is then explained, and a case example given.

The reason for this chosen format is that it may take time for the newly qualified Healer to become sufficiently experienced to respond to the conditions in a spontaneous way, and rather than having to search the texts for specific practical guidance, it would be much simpler to be able to identify conditions in the texts, although for completeness some are duplicated from previous pages.

The healing methods given in this book are so straight forward and simple that it is best for the Healer to proceed with them in the form given. In rare cases however, there may be some less obvious factor playing a part in the subject's condition.

THE 'MEDICAL' ENQUIRY METHOD

If a presenting condition has a psychological origin, the healing methods put forward may be less effective until that factor is resolved. Preferably a competent analytical hypnotherapist should be engaged to provide this service.

Then too, if the condition reported is the result of bodily misuse, lack of exercise, poor diet, the side effects of medication or bad posture (a 'bad back' for instance, can often be caused by this last example) then these factors call for consideration and correction too.

With so many possibilities the need to identify them arises, but take heart for the subconscious mind parts will know the truth, and they can be asked to provide that information using the following method.

Take the subject into hypnosis and inform the subject's subconscious that you have been requested by the subject to assist him with the condition that distresses him, and that in order to be of assistance some further information is required. The subconscious is asked to provide that information initially as 'yes' or 'no' answers.

For this the subconscious should cause a green light effect in the subject's mind for 'yes', and a red for 'no', or that the subconscious should cause a physical response in the subject's right eye for 'yes' and in the left eye for 'no', ensuring the subject is made aware of which is his right eye by touching his right hand whilst saying, 'the right eye is the eye on this side'. Whichever method of signalling is to be used, the subconscious is requested to make the reaction spontaneously and distinctly.

AN EXAMPLE OF THE MEDICAL ENQUIRY METHOD IN PRACTICE

Hypnosis has been induced, and the subject's subconscious has been instructed in the responses it should give to the questions to be asked.

Healer: "Subconscious, Peter reports to me that he suffers with poor general health. Subconscious, please carry out a thorough medical examination of him and say 'yes' when you have."

Note, in such a general examination the reported 'yes' signal may take twenty seconds or more to arrive, should it go beyond that time the subconscious could be asked to provide the 'yes' signal to confirm that the examination is continuing. Should the subconscious fail to provide this confirmation, further negotiations are to be proceeded with. In this later case either the subconscious has not understood its role in the exercise, or be more likely that the condition has a psychological origin that the subconscious is reluctant to risk exposing. In this case negotiations are again called for, and in the rare case of failure, analysis is called for.

Assuming the 'yes' signal has been given by Peter's subconscious, the 'medical' enquiry would then continue thus.

Healer: "Thank you subconscious. Subconscious, is Peter's poor general health caused by a psychological factor?"

Peter: "Yes".

Healer: "Thank you subconscious. Subconscious, Peter needs to know what that psychological factor is, I shall count to three, click my fingers and you pass that information to Peter then." (one, two, three click).

Peter: (Beginning to weep) "I hate my boss at work and my wife doesn't try to help me, and the stress is causing me to be unwell."

A FURTHER EXAMPLE

At a talk I gave, a member of the audience questioned my explanation of the mind's ability to check the body. It was an embarrassing moment, for in the midst of my talk I had effectively been faced with the confrontational 'prove it' demand. I must confess, thrown off my course by such an unexpected challenging response, I felt a little angry. Immediately I invited him to come forward for the method to be demonstrated on him. Enthusiastically he came forward, I suspect to impress the audience by proving me wrong.

Some mockery of him by other audience members took place as he came forward, who seemed to hold him in contempt for interrupting the proceedings. Wishing to demonstrate my independence, I asked for a volunteer to act as my assistant for the hand holding technique. (In this technique a third person is called for to hold the subjects right hand, and for the subject's subconscious to indicate 'yes' responses by causing a nerve in that hand to react that can be felt by both parties, and for nothing to be done to represent 'no'.)

Much amusement now ensued as an extraordinarily attractive female came forward in response. Further outcries from the audience took place as she took his hand as I had instructed her to, following the induction of hypnosis. The male volunteer was clearly elated with the female holding his hand, and given the circumstances there seemed little chance of success - or so I thought.

I asked the male volunteer, lets call him Arnold, and the female assistant Ann, what part of his body he wanted to be checked. "My lungs", he replied in front of the now quietened audience of some sixty members. The following was to take place after I had instructed Arnold's subconscious on how it should respond.

Me.   "Subconscious, Arnold has asked me to ask you to conduct an examination of his lungs, would you send the 'yes' signal to indicate your willingness to do so?"

Ann.   (Surprised and smiling) reported the 'yes' signal had been given.

Me: "Thank you subconscious, then please examine Arnold's right lung and signal 'yes' when you have".

Ann.   (Again smiling - and in only some seven seconds later.) "Yes".

Me: "Subconscious, do you find Arnold's right lung to be healthy and fit?"

Ann: "Yes - I got a 'yes' signal!"

Me: "Thank you subconscious, please carry out an examination of Arnold's left lung now and again signal 'yes' when you have."

By now my confidence in the success of the demonstration was rapidly being restored. However that confidence in a successful demonstration soon began to be replaced by apprehension. The seconds were ticking by, and the delay in the 'yes' signal could only indicate that something was wrong with Arnold's left lung, and I had set myself up to having to reveal that fact to one and all, in public. Some forty seconds later came the 'yes' signal, but nobody but me could have realised what that delay indicated.

Ann.   (Looking curious) "Yes, I got yes!"

Me.   "Subconscious, do you find Arnold's left lung to be healthy and fit?"

Ann.   (Following a pause) "I didn't get a yes".

Me.   (My fears mounting) 'Then subconscious do you find something to be wrong with Arnold's left lung?"

Ann   (Looking very serious) "I got yes!"

Me   "Arnold, do you smoke?"

Arnold "No, but you've proved your point and I'm amazed. You see about a year ago I broke a rib and it penetrated my left lung, I'm recovering well, but it still hurts a bit and you found it."

Wild applause from the audience. Immense relief for myself and a good lesson learned.

A CURIOSITY

A question often asked is, since the healing methods used are so simple and often instant, 'why does the healing not take place as part of normal bodily maintenance?' Well mostly it does of course. After all if a bone is fractured it will normally be healed naturally, you may need splints or a plaster casing to assist that healing, but it will be healed naturally and without medication.

Then if you work manually hard with your hands, the skin will be thickened to protect them. If we suffer a wound the arteries supplying the area will rapidly constrict to reduce blood loss. If we become too hot we will pinken, as the blood flows nearer the skin surface to loose heat, and when we are cold the reverse happens and we become pale, Should something get into an eye the eye will respond by producing fluid to wash it away.

In the course of a fever our temperatures rise in an attempt to kill the invading bacteria with heat. Eating badly contaminated food will cause messages to be sent to the centre of the brain, and then internal messages will be sent to the nerves servicing the muscles of the abdomen, which are normally only used for breathing, as a result the stomach comes under considerable pressure and the offending food will be ejected with speed.

There are hundreds if not thousands of further examples of our inbuilt mechanisms for healing and bodily maintenance. So, to repeat the question in another way, why does arthritis and so many other bodily conditions not respond in a similar fashion? Well, nobody in the medical world that I have asked seems to know.

Mostly those asked suggest that its probably because these conditions have a virus causing them and that this can be more difficult for the body to deal with. Yet as far as I know, no such virus, despite decades of intensive research, has ever been identified in any of the two hundred named variations of arthritis.

Although it must be said that some infections are known to trigger arthritis, but even then, it still poses the question as to why arthritis triggered in this way continues, even after the infection has been dealt with.

At a meeting with a general medical practice the question was posed to me in reverse. "How can", asked one Doctor, "a patient be apparently instantly relieved of arthritis who has suffered for years with it?" He then went on to explain the mechanisms that would be necessary in some detail. At first I listened to his explanations intently and began to realise that it must be impossible.

An alarm bell suddenly sounded in my mind. I was beginning to allow myself to believe, by the sheer logic of his medical argument, that the instant relief could not occur. Then I realised that here was a Doctor who could not successfully treat arthritis, telling me who could, why I couldn't, and that if I continued to listen to him I might be converted to his views, doubt myself and perhaps hinder my success rates. Then it flashed into my mind that by all the theories of aviation and flight borne craft, the bee can't fly. Happily everyone but the bee knows this, and he, in his ignorance, continues to fly.

THE JOURNEY AHEAD

Come with me then on our journey ahead, down the path leading to healing skills that will amaze you too. It makes no difference if you should doubt your ability to heal in the ways to be described, for you can. For the

59

journey you may take with you as much scepticism as you can carry, but along the route, and bit by bit, you will discard it among the heaps of scepticism discarded on their way, by the hundreds of those who have trod the path before you. Should you struggle with your load to the end of the journey, then you can start a pile of discarded scepticism for yourself, with the amazing effects of just having the little confidence to try the healing methods for yourself.

That journey has already commenced, and the journey is soon to be completed through the pages ahead, as we learn what has to be known for the harvest of success awaiting and beckoning us. Who knows how many lives you will then change for the better, what satisfaction you will enjoy and what rewards you will reap?

PART FOUR

CONDITIONS AND TREATMENT METHODS

ARTHRITIS

There are over two hundred named arthritic conditions, but we need not feel unduly daunted by this, since these, in general, are names given to the location of the condition, spondylitis, for instance is the term used to describe arthritis in the spine. Some arthritic conditions may also be referred to as this or that being 'frozen'. More importantly we need to recognise the three principle types of arthritis, and to understand the general nature of each. Collectively the term arthritis can be said to mean the inflammation, stiffness, painfulness or distortion of joints.

The three principle types of arthritis are Osteo-arthritis, Rheumatoid arthritis and Gout.

OSTEO-ARTHRITIS

This is a gradual or more rapid deterioration of one or more joints, in which the cartilage, a gristle like substance becomes eroded or depleted. It is important for our work to think of the cartilage as a protective film which lines the bones at the point of contact in the joints and between muscles. In osteo-arthritis rough deposits of bone often occur as the cartilage degenerates.

HEALING OSTEO-ARTHRITIS

Where several bodily areas are affected it is best to restrict the healing to two at each session. Though in the case of multiple joints in the same area, they can be treated together at a single session, the spine, hands and feet are examples. The reasons for this restriction are that it helps focus the mind more effectively on the treated part, and therefore tends to produce superior results. Additionally some time may be required for the subject to latch on to the healing method being used initially, and particularly where a subject claims to lack visualisation.

Then too, the Healer should be aware that, rather like a battery can be, his healing 'charge' may run down in prolonged use, especially where he has had to adopt an uncomfortable bodily position himself to render the healing. A further benefit of restricting the healing conducted, particularly where a subject is highly sceptical, as some are to begin with, is that it can help enormously to increase that subject's enthusiasm if, say, one of two affected knees only is treated, with the subject now able to feel the difference between the two as a result. In this the objective is not to leave one knee in pain, but to help assist motivation by demonstrating what can be achieved.

TREATING OSTEO-ARTHRITIS

The subject will normally have had his condition diagnosed as osteo-arthritis, leaving the Healer to decide only on whether the condition is more likely to be some factor of the neglect of the base subconscious or the deliberate result of the intermediate mind.

This is normally much simpler than it sounds. Generally speaking, if the subject reports that the condition has gradually emerged over time, that he can't be too sure when it started, can think of no serious personal set backs having occurred, and is in other respects reasonably contented with life, then the negligence factor can be suspected. The treatment can begin.

If however, the subject reports that the condition developed quite quickly, even 'overnight', and particularly following some significant emotional event, then the intermediate subconscious mind can be suspected as the area for the initial healing, since this is often an indication of a psychological factor. Especially should this be confirmed by the enquiry method, then analysis is called for, although the healing may still be attempted.

Significant emotional events could include divorce, redundancy, bereavement, bankruptcy, failure in some important endeavour, an accident, a major disappointment, shock or setback. Also to be included are happy and exciting events, the birth of a child, marriage, promotion or some outstanding achievement as examples.

Should there be any doubt as to whether the intermediate or base subconscious minds are the causual factor, it does no harm to direct the initial attempt at healing in the manner which follows. Firstly explain to the subject exactly what you intend to do. A simple explanation with no medical terms is enough. You could proceed by telling the subject what is to be done is as follows.

Healer: "Shortly I shall help you to relax, because whilst you are relaxed you wil be able to concentrate better. Then, when you are more relaxed, I shall sit beside you with one hand under (or just below) and with the other on top (or just above) your knee. When I have done that, I shall invite you to imagine that you are looking inside your knee and seeing some part of it. You may not have a photographic like picture come into your mind, but you will be able to imagine yourself visualising something."

Check with the subject that he understands his role. Following his confirmation relax the subject into hypnosis using the methods described earlier. Having relaxed the subject, sit with him with your hands located in the way you explained to him.

Following this, encourage him to imagine some picture. With a little patience and encouragement some visual picture can be expected to emerge. Quite often he will report imagining some bone structure, or some tissue being discoloured or swollen.

In this example of an osteo-arthritic knee, the subject can be expected to report imagining some bone structure. He should be asked what colour he imagines the bone to be, when he responds, he should be asked if the reported colour is the correct one for that bone to be healthy and fit. Should he say 'no' he should be asked what colour it should be, and most respond that it should be silver blue, pinkish, white or ivory.

Following this the subject should be asked how he could imagine changing the colour to the correct one. Sometimes he will report that the colour is changing to the correct one as he watches it, in this case he should be asked to report when the colour is correct. Alternatively, should he say that he doesn't know how to change it, some suggestions or options should be given. He may be asked if he could imagine cleaning it, painting it or applying some magical cream for example.

Where the bone structure visualised is reported to be correct, or has been reported as corrected, the subject should be asked to report on the structural condition of the bones in the knee area. A common response is a report of roughness, pitting, wear or erosion.

In such cases the subject should be asked how he could imagine rectifying the structure. Should his response be that he does not know how to rectify it, then again some suggestions or options should be offered. He might imagine himself sanding or filing it down. As a further option he may imagine it correcting itself.

In cases of wear, pitting or erosion, he might imagine himself applying some fine strong cement mix. One method I find to be both popular and highly effective, is to ask the subject if he is familiar with the modern method a dentist uses to fill front teeth. He may say 'yes' or respond that he doesn't. In either case I run through the principles of the method, because this helps his subconscious mind to focus on the healing itself more clearly.

It doesn't matter if he should subsequently select an alternative, because should he do so, his subconscious will have been given two illustrations of what needs to be done to heal. I usually describe the dental method along the following lines.

Healer: "In modern times the dentist uses a malleable filling which can be colour matched to his patients teeth. This remains soft whilst the dentist applies it. Having done this the dentist then uses a torch-like device which emits an ultra violet light. This light has the effect of hardening the filling until it is even harder and stronger than the tooth, which in turn is the hardest bone structure in the body."

Mostly this option to fill pitted, worn or eroded bone will be accepted. Whichever method is selected, the subject should be guided through the chosen method, while keeping the Healer constantly informed of the progress being visualised.

Of all conditions reported by subjects being treated for arthritis, by far the most common is the perceived dryness of the bone structure in the affected joint. So important is this aspect of treating arthritis that, even where the effected joint is reported to be lubricated, I take no chances. Suggest to the subject that there should be a pipe somewhere in the effected area that brings the oil to the joint.

Ask him to imagine himself finding it and then holding the end of it. He might imagine it as a hose pipe, a plastic tube, or as taking some other form. Next ask him if any oil is coming out, if he says 'yes', ask if its enough, if he reports that it is, ask him to imagine feeling the oil with his fingers, and to tell you if the quality or density is correct.

Normally some deficiency will be reported, but more commonly he will report that little or no oil is emerging. When this is reported to be the case, he should imagine himself checking the end of the pipe to make sure that its not blocked. In some cases he will imagine that it is.

Following such a report he could be asked to see himself clearing it, using something to poke it clear, failing this he could imagine himself turning the tap on to a higher pressure to clear the pipe, and then watch the oil emerging. As a further alternative he could imagine replacing the pipe, in whole or part, or simply check that the pipe is not trapped, twisted or caught up in some way.

Should the pipe be reported to be alright, on reaching the tap, the tap should be imagined being turned on to full. In rare cases where this tap process fails, the subject should be guided further back to the local mains tap, the general distribution tap, and ultimately to the oil production source. In all of this, the subject is to be encouraged to imagine himself turning any closed taps back on, and if all are on, to carry out alterations, adjustments or repairs to the production source.

In this latter case, he could imagine some valve stuck, the production unit not switched on, or imagine himself adjusting the controls of the production unit. Often the subject will have his own suggestions, such as exchanging some unit, the entire production source, or switching on an auxiliary unit for examples. Where the quality of the oil is reported as deficient or poor, the pipe should be followed back to the mixture valves supplying the tap. These valves should then be adjusted until the quality of the oil has been restored.

When the oil is reported to be flowing in the correct quantity and quality, ensure that the oil is being delivered to the joint. This can be achieved by suggesting to the subject that he finds some groove, channel or input point in the joint, that the pipe fits into exactly and firmly. When this is imagined the pipe should be visualised as being fitted. The subject should then be encouraged to imagine himself looking inside the joint, and watching it fill with the oil.

He is to watch it as it seeps into every crevice, and gently emerging to moisten the exterior surface too. When this has also been imagined, suggest that, without actually moving the joint, he can imagine it moving like some precision engineered part, well oiled and moving smoothly and perfectly. Following the report that it has been imagined working this way, he should then be asked to actually move it to test it.

Expect your subject, and not least yourself, to be amazed at the result. Exactly the same procedure illustrated for treating an osteo-arthritic knee, can be used for a foot, ankle, hip, hand, wrist, elbow, shoulder, neck or spinal condition. However in 'oiling' a spinal condition it is good practice to have the subject imagining the oil being delivered to the top of the spinal column, and seeping down the entire structure. It is also a good idea, especially in this case, to incorporate the concept of healthy nutrients being mixed in with the oil.

Where the hands are actually placed in contact with the joint to be healed, and the subject is of the opposite sex, it is best to be accompanied by a member of the subjects own sex, unless the subject is a close friend or relative, especially if some clothing needs to be adjusted, such as the raising of a skirt when treating a knee. Note too that whilst the four fingers are naturally aligned the thumb is not, consequently the thumb can have a tendency to 'wander' and could give rise to false impressions if this is not realised.

OSTEO-ARTHRITIS A TREATMENT EXAMPLE

The subject has an osteo-arthritic knee to be treated, the procedure has been explained and the subject relaxed into hypnosis, the Healer is sitting with the subject with his hands placed on the knee, and has just asked for the visualised picture.

Subject. "I can imagine a bone."

Healer. "Good! What do you notice about it?"

Subject. "How do you mean?"

Healer. "Well, what colour is it?"

Subject: "It's very red and looks sore."

Healer: "What colour would it be if it wasn't sore?"

Subject. "A sort of creamy white."

Healer. "How could you change it to creamy white?"

Subject. "I don't know!"

Healer. "Could you imagine painting it, or just watch it turn creamy white?"

Subject: "I could wipe it better with a soft cloth with some cream on it."

Healer. "Then see yourself doing that and keep me informed of your progress."

Subject. "It's working, its working!"

Healer: "Tell me when its a nice creamy white."

Subject. "It looks O.K. now!"

Healer. "Does it still look sore?"

Subject: "Yes, a bit, its been rubbing on another bone."

Healer. "What's causing it to rub?"

Subject. "I don't know."

Healer. "Look at the point of contact, and tell me if there's a good film of oil between them."

Subject. "No, it's all dry, pitted and rough."

Healer. "How could you make those bones smooth."

Subject. "I'll sandpaper them smooth."

Healer. "Tell me when they are all nice and smooth."

Subject. "It is coming on well - I've done it."

Healer. "Good, are the bones still pitted?"

Subject. "A bit."

Healer. "How could you fill that pitting?"

Subject. "I could fill them with strong glue that sets very hard."

Healer. "Do that and keep telling me how its progressing."

Subject. "I've done it already, I scratched the glue with my nail and its very hard already."

Healer. "There should be a pipe there somewhere that brings the oil for the knee, tell me when you've found it and imagining holding it in your hand."

Subject. "I've got it."

Healer. "Is any oil coming out?"

Subject. "No."

Healer. "Check if the end is blocked. Poke something into it perhaps."

Subject. "No, it's not blocked."

Healer. "Check that the pipes not twisted or trapped - follow it all the way back to the tap if you need to."

Subject. "It seems O.K"

Healer. "Check if the tap is turned on."

Subject. "No it's rusted up but I think I can work it free and turn it on."

Healer. "Tell me what happens."

Subject. "Oh! There's a lot of oil flowing, the pipe spluttered at first but the oil is coming out now."

Healer. "Test the oil with your thumb and finger, then tell me if it seems a good quality oil."

Subject. "No, it's too thin."

Healer. "Then go back to the tap and adjust the mixing valves supplying the tap, tell me when you've done that."

Subject. "Yes, I've done that and the mixture is fine now."

Healer. "Good, there's a groove or channel leading into the joint, that the pipe will fit into firmly, I want you to find that grove or channel, and ease the pipe into it so that the oil flows into the knee joint. Tell me when you have done that and what's happening."

Subject. "It's fixed, the oil has filled the joint nicely."

Healer. "Now without actually moving the knee joint, imagine that you were, and watch as it moves like some precision engineering part, see how the oil covers and protects every part. Tell me when you've imagined that too."

Subject. (Smiling) "It's O.K. - it's good."

Healer. "Excellent. I'm taking my hands away and I'd like you to test your knee by moving it."

Subject. (Smiling broadly or looking amazed) "I don't believe it, its back to normal!"

Note: As in all similar treatments, where the subject reports very little or even no imagined pictures, a similar exercise can be conducted but with the Healer explaining what he is imagining doing, whilst the subject concentrates on what the Healer says.

RHEUMATOID ARTHRITIS

This form of Arthritis mainly effects the smaller joints of hands and feet, with mostly all the joints in the area being involved in the condition. Women are five times more likely to be sufferers than men. In more acute cases the condition may be accompanied by variable fatigue or fever and anaemia or weight loss. Muscles can also deteriorate, producing deformity and restricted movement resulting from muscle contractions. The fusing of joints or partial dislocations can also occur. Serious crippling can result in addition to severe pain.

TREATING RHEUMATOID ARTHRITIS

The victim of this condition can also be expected to have had medical confirmation of it. However, perhaps even more importantly, the essential need for medical attention should be stressed, especially since there are strong indications that infection or toxaemia could be present

The treatment for this condition should also include the methods given for treating osteo-arthritis. However, in rheumatoid arthritis, and not infrequently in osteo-arthritis, affected tissue, muscles, tendons, nerves or blood vessels can be expected to be reported or imagined. Such a report might include faulty colouring, tension, twisting, entrapment, restrictions, undue slackness, roughness or some part not being strong or big enough. In all cases the Healer should ask his subject how he could imagine correcting reported faults.

Again some suggestions and options might be required. Such suggestions and options might include the subject imagining himself cleaning some part, painting it the correct colour, gently working in some selected or magical healing cream. Mechanical actions, like adjusting nuts, screws or fasteners might be employed. Faulty parts can be imagined as being replaced by new and perfect parts.

Increasing size and strengthening parts can be imagined by visualising them being massaged, perhaps incorporating some health producing oil or cream. With just a little imagination a simple solution can be put to the subject for him to work on. An essential part of the healing, where physical distortion has resulted, is to have the subject visualise the restoration of realigning the effected area.

In particular, muscles should be visualised as expanding back to their original strength and size. By the very nature of this condition, repeated sessions of treatment may well be called for. In both forms of osteo and rheumatoid arthritis cases, an entire limb, or more than one will need to be treated. To avoid over-taxing the Healer and the subject alike, each healing session should be restricted to treating a single limb where more than one is affected.

RHEUMATOID ARTHRITIS A TREATMENT EXAMPLE

In this example the subject has been given the advice of the treatment method to come, as put forward for osteo-arthritis, taken into hypnosis and been guided through the osteo-arthritis oiling procedure.

The stage has now been reached where the treatment is to be specifically directed at the rheumatoidal symptoms.

The subject has a painful and distorted right hand, and the Healer is seated by the subject's side, sandwiching it with his hands.

Healer   "I want you to imagine that you are looking inside your hand and to tell me what you notice about the structure of it"

Subject.   "It's all distorted, weak looking and inflamed."

Healer.   "Let's tackle the inflammation first, how could you do that?"

Note.   By this stage the subject should have a good understanding of the healing method, and especially where benefits have been experienced from the previous oiling session, and now be ready and able to anticipate more readily and spontaneously.

Subject. "I can apply a magical soothing and healing cream - I'm doing that now."

Healer. "Tell me what is now happening."

Subject. "It's looking better and becoming pinker."

Healer. "Tell me when it looks healthy."

Subject. "It looks much better now, and my hand is tingling a bit."

Healer. "Fine, the tingling is an indication of the healing taking place, so tell me when your ready to work on strengthening the structure."

Subject. "How can I do that?"

Healer. "I could gently make small massaging movements with my hand as you watch it begin to look stronger, shall we try that?"

Subject. "Yes".

Healer   "Now keep looking at it as I massage it, and let me know what's happening."

Subject. "The blood is circulating better, the muscles are expanding and becoming stronger."

Healer. "Good. Lets keep going until your hand is strong again."

Subject. "My hand feels very warm and looks much stronger already."

Healer. "Good, the warmth in your hand is a further indication that it is becoming stronger, healthier and fitter."

Subject. "I can feel my hand becoming stronger."

Healer. "Good, keep working on it until your ready to test it."

Subject. "Lets test it now." (Healer removes his hands and watches the test as the subject flexes his hand.)

Subject. "It feels much stronger, but it's not back to as it was before the arthritis."

Healer. "We shall need to work on it some more later, but I want to help that process by starting to realign the hand. I will hold it again."

Subject. "O.K., what shall I do next?"

Healer. "Select a finger (or thumb) to work on, and tell me which one you have chosen."

Subject. "My first finger, the one next to my thumb."

Healer. "Right, then begin to see those strengthened muscles pulling it into alignment and keep telling me how it's going."

Subject. "I can imagine it beginning to straighten, but it's slow."

Healer. "Keep going, your getting there."

Subject. "I'm feeling something happen and my hand feels strange."

Healer. "Fine, that's another indication of healing, tell me when you can imagine that finger to be straightened."

Subject "Yes, I can imagine that now."

Note: the process is then repeated for the other fingers, thumbs and, where appropriate, the wrist, which in any case should be oiled. At the end of each session the Healer should physically exercise the subject's hands. A good way is for the palms of both to be brought into contact, fingers touching, with the subject holding his hand out in much the same way a policeman holds his hand to stop traffic, but holding the hand slightly lower. When in this position, a gentle pressure is applied by the subject to the Healer's hand, with small movements taking place.

Only limited, if any restoration to deformity may occur, but some may. Not only this, but it can be expected that the condition will no longer deteriorate further, and the subject should be told to make more effort to exercise that part to further strengthen it. A further good idea is for the subject to be taught self-hypnosis and to use it to visualise enhanced improvement taking place.

GOUT

Gout is the result of excess uric acid in the blood stream, producing deposits of sodium urate in the cartilage of the joints, and sometimes in the ears. This condition normally responds well to conventional medicine but the Healer can assist too. The subject can be asked, in hypnosis, to imagine himself looking at some part responsible for producing the sodium urate, with a view to adjusting the controls on that part. In addition the subject may visualise the dissolving of the sodium urate. A psychological cause should also be considered, much in the way as illustrated for diabetes.

PART FIVE

LIMB & BODY HEALING

LIMB AND BODILY CONDITIONS

In this part of the text non arthritic conditions, such as sprains, bruises, dislocations, pains, weakened parts, accidents and helping with surgical recovery are described. For brevity of presentation, the explanation to the subject that he is to imagine himself carrying out repairs and alterations, and the subject having been taken into hypnosis is assumed.

BRUISES

A bruise may be defined as an injury caused by impact without breaking the skin, causing blood to be excreted into the tissue. Discoloration changes as the blood of the bruise begins to breakdown and becomes re-absorbed. Often commencing as dark red or purplish, over a week or so the bruise may change to various shades of brown and green, and appear pale yellow before disappearing.

The simple healing method to follow normally greatly speeds the process, and the colour changes can occur within hours rather than days. Medically a cold damp cloth, and where the pain has lessoned, gentle massaging can help speed recovery. However, and especially since bruises can be painful and sensitive, the natural healing method can be applied without any physical contact.

THE BRUISE HEALING METHOD

In a similar way as much of our rapid natural healing is conducted, the subject is to imagine himself inside the area and simply washing or cleaning it. The earlier in the colour change sequence that the method is used the greater the benefit will be, with little if any advantages at the pale yellow stage, unless concern exists from the visual effect, say of a bruised face.

BRUISE HEALING EXAMPLE

Healer. "Tell me when you can imagine yourself inside the bruised area and looking at what its like."

Subject. "I can imagine a dark red swollen area."

Healer. "What can you do to make it look better?"

Subject. "I don't know."

Healer. "As you know, the bruise is made up of blood that has escaped during impact, so could you try imagining yourself washing it away, say with a hose pipe?"

Subject. "Yes, I'll do that, I'll imagine it's like washing mud off a wall."

Healer. "Good, keep imagining it all being washed away. There are some drains in there, see everything that's being washed off flowing into them and keep me in touch with how you're getting on."

Subject. "It's all washing away nicely and becoming lighter."

Healer. "Good, tell me when you imagine it to be clean."

Subject. "That's it, it looks nice and clean."

Healer. "How does it feel?"

Subject. "Still a bit swollen and tender."

Healer. "Would it help to imagine a fan blowing cool air into that area to reduce the swelling and make it more comfortable?"

Subject. "No, I'll pack it with ice, that will fix it."

Healer. "Good, tell me when you have."

Subject. "I've done it, and its feeling much better now thank you."

BACK ACHE AND BACK CONDITIONS

These can have many causes and between them they constitute a major cause of disability and suffering. Since there is a possibility of infection in the kidneys, an abscess or a malignant disease of any organ in such conditions, the advice to ensure that medical attention is sought is further underscored. Other factors contributing to these conditions can include a bone disease, such as osseous tuberculosis, osteo-arthritis, a prolapsed inter-vertebral disc, (more commonly known as a slipped disc) lumbago, fibrositis or muscular rheumatism, back strain, ligament damage, trapped nerves and vertebra defects, such as spondylitis (spinal inflammation) and spondylosis (joint fixation) can also be causes.

However, and especially where medical attention has been received, no harm can come from conducting the attempted relief of a given back condition by using the methods to follow.

A BACK STRAIN HEALING EXAMPLE

Healer. "Now imagine that you are looking at the area of discomfort, but from the inside of it, and tell me what you notice."

Subject. "I can imagine a large dark red area."

Healer. "O.K., should it be dark red?"

Subject. "I don't think so."

Healer. "What colour should it be to be fit and comfortable?"

Subject "A light red I think."

Healer. "How can you change it to light red?"

Subject. "I could rub some powdered ice into it."

Healer. "Good, do that and tell me how its reacting."

Subject. "It's becoming a lighter red already, its feeling easier too.....and tingling a bit."

Healer. "Good, tell me when the colour has become light red."

Subject. "It looks light red now, but it seems a bit tight and strained still."

76

Healer "If you could imagine massaging in some light healing oil or cream would that help ease it?"

Subject. "Yes, that's what I'll do, and I'm doing it now."

Healer. "Good, imagine you can see all the fibres relaxing and gently slipping into their proper places, easily and smoothly. Keep going until it's all fit and well again."

Subject. "I've done all that and it is much easier already."

SLIPPED DISC

This is often a very painful condition that occurs when the cartilaginous disc between the vertebras become displaced, or emits some of its jelly like content, causing pressure on the nerves in the spinal column. The pain may be experienced in the effected area, some organ, or in muscles served by the nerves subjected to the pressure - such as can happen with sciatica, where pain is experienced in the calf or thigh.

During the treatment, and where possible, the healer is to hold a hand on the effected back part. Prior to commencing the treatment it can help the subject carry out the healing, by the healer explaining the general nature of the cause of the condition. This is especially important in cases such as sciatica, where the subject may feel that the treatment should be directed specifically at the area of actual pain.

A SLIPPED DISC HEALING EXAMPLE

The subject having understood his role is in hypnosis, and with the Healer holding his hand on the effected back part.

Healer. "I want you to imagine that you are looking at the area effected, but from inside, and tell me what you are imagining."

Subject. "There is a dark blob pressing on a red cord and causing the pain."

Healer. "How could you imagine changing that to make it well again?"

Subject. "I don't know, and it looks as if the bones are touching too, because so much of the jelly has leaked out."

Healer. "Would it help if you imagined yourself dissolving the blob with some penetrating oil or cream?"

Subject. "I'll try that.......but it's taking some time to melt away."

Healer. "Keep me in touch with your progress."

Subject. "It's coming on now, and my back is very warm where you are holding your hand."

Healer. "Good, tell me when the blob has melted away"

Subject. "It's gone! My back feels much better and the cord has become pinker."

Healer. "And what colour should the cord be to be completely healthy and fit."

Subject. "Bluish I think."

Healer. "How can you make it that good bluish colour?"

Subject. "It's becoming a nice bluish colour as I watch it, it's a nice bluish colour now."

Healer. "I want you to look at the point where the jelly escaped and tell me what you imagine."

Subject "There's a small hole in it."

Healer. "How could you fix that?"

Subject. "I'll fill it with some strong glue....that's it, it looks good."

Healer. "You said the bones seemed to be touching, would it be a good idea to refill the disc so that it moved the bones apart?"

Subject. "Yes, but how?"

Healer. "You know how grease is injected using a hand grease pump, you could imagine using that on the greasing nipples on each side of the disc, inflating it a bit on one side and then the other, watching it becoming fuller as you do, and seeing the bones gradually being restored to their proper position."

Subject. "Yes, yes, I'm doing that, and I can see them parting. That's good, it's done."

Healer. "Do you notice anything about the muscles in the area?"

Subject. "Oh Yes, they look weakened."

Healer. "Could you strengthen them by imagining yourself plumping them up like we do with pillows and cushions?"

Subject. "Yes, I'm doing that and they look a better pink colour as well as looking stronger already."

Healer. Tell me when they are all healthy and strong."

Subject. "I've done it, it looks good and all the pain has gone, it feels normal now."

Note. Following this, should some pain be reported to be continuing in some other area, as the result of the slipped disc, then the visualisation of healing that should also be conducted, where possible with a hand or hands held on the area of discomfort. The treatment could be as in the following example.

Healer. "Imagine you are looking inside the area and tell me what you are looking at."

Subject. "I can see a sore red nerve and the muscle round it looks inflamed."

Healer. "With the methods we have been using how could you correct that."

Subject. "I'll gently apply some easing cream in the area."

Healer. "Tell me what happens."

Subject. "It's easing, feeling better and looking more relaxed."

Healer. "Tell me when its done."

Subject. "That's it, but I think I'll plump the muscles up too."

Healer. "Tell me when you have and how it feels."

Subject. "It's done and it feels fine now."

LUMBAGO

This is a general term for pain in the small of the back, with any of a diversity of causes. These can include lumber strain, arthritis and a slipped disc as examples. The pain may be severe and with the subject unable to straighten his back. Because of the variety of possible causes, a medical diagnosis is a pre-requisite for using the healing methods set out. The relevant healing methods described for treating arthritis, back strain and slipped disc should be employed.

FIBROSITIS

Another term for this condition is muscular rheumatism, and effecting both joints and muscles, producing pain, tenderness and muscular stiffness. Mental stress, being exposed to cold air and kidney infections can be some of the causes, and again call for a medical diagnosis. Where exposure to cold air has been the cause, warming the area can help, together with keeping the back better protected. In suitable cases, that is in non infection fibrositis, healing can be conducted with the subject being asked to carry out self-healing in the manner illustrated for back strain. However, rather than using powdered ice, some heating or warming substance should be employed, such as a muscle easing cream.

TRAPPED NERVES

These can occur in many points of the body, and the methods of treating them are the same as in the examples to follow for treating trapped nerves in the back and wrist. It should be borne in mind that a trapped nerve may cause pain or disability in a part even remote to the point of entrapment, again such as in sciatica.

TRAPPED NERVE HEALING EXAMPLES

In the first example the subject has reported that the pain he has been experiencing in his right leg and foot has been diagnosed as sciatica. Medical examinations have discounted a slipped disc, osteo-arthritis or disease within the pelvis. The subject has been prescribed analgesics to help with the pain, and an exploratory operation has been suggested in his lower back in the area of the lumber vertebrae and sacrum, the wedge shaped bone at the base of the spine. The subject, having had his role explained, is in hypnosis with the Healer sitting with his hand on the area affected, the Healer begins his therapy.

Healer. "I want you to imagine that you are looking at the area that I have my hand on, but from inside it, and tell me what you are imagining yourself seeing."

Subject. "I'm not sure, but it looks like some knobbly bones."

Healer. "Keep looking at them, examine the area and tell me if you notice anything."

Subject. "Yes, there's a red cord."

Healer. "Should it be red?"

Subject. "No, there's something wrong with it, and I think it's inflamed."

Healer. "O.K., what's causing it to be red and inflamed?"

Subject. "I don't know."

Healer. "Imagine yourself tracing the red cord back towards the knobbly-bones, and tell me if you can imagine seeing what's causing it to be red and inflamed."

Subject. "I'm imagining it to be squeezed somehow, I think it's in the wrong place too."

Healer. "How could you ease it into the correct position?"

Subject. "It looks tight too but I can't think of what to do."

Healer. "Well, could you see yourself gently applying some soothing cream to help slacken it, and make it slippy enough for you to be able to slide it, bit by bit, into its right place?"

Subject. "Yes, I'll do that."

Healer. "Good, keep telling me what happens."

Subject. "I'm putting the cream on with my index finger, and its already looking less red and inflamed. My back feels nice and warm where your hand is."

81

Healer. "Good, the warmth is a sign of the healing becoming affective. Now, when you are ready begin easing the cord into the correct position."

Subject. "Yes I'm doing that........and it is moving......ah!" (Subject flinches).

Healer. "What happened just then?"

Subject. (Smiling) "Its O.K., it suddenly clicked into place and made me jump for a moment, but it looks good now and the inflammation has gone and the cord looks a creamy blue colour.... there's no pain in my leg either!"

Healer. "Excellent, now check around the area for anything else which might need attention, such as some muscle tissue, and look for anything else which might be in the wrong place."

Subject. "No, everything seems fine and I feel a lot better now, thank you."

A FURTHER TRAPPED NERVE
HEALING EXAMPLE

In the following example the subject reports that his Doctor thinks that the pain in his wrist and hand could be the result of a dislocated or trapped nerve resulting from a car accident he has had. Analgesics have been prescribed pending a visit to a consultant. However, with the pain, and not being able to use his hand, the subject feels he can't wait and is seeking earlier relief. The subject understands his role, and is in hypnosis with the Healer sitting holding the subject's wrist with both hands.

Healer. "I want you to imagine that you can see inside your wrist, look around it and tell me what you notice."

Subject. "It looks dark brown and tense."

Healer. "What colour should it be not to be tense?"

Subject. "Pink I think."

Healer. "So what's causing it to be brown and tense?"

Subject. "It's the nerves - I can see a big one that looks twisted and caught over a small piece of bone."

Healer. "Right, what can you do to untwist it and free it from being caught over that small bone?"

Subject. "It's been twisted over the bone, so if I use a very fine lever I could try levering it off and it will be untwisted at the same time."

Healer. "Good, do that and tell me what happens."

Subject. "It won't budge, it won't budge!"

Healer. "Would it help if you oiled or creamed the area to make it slippier?"

Subject "Yes.....it's moving, it's moving!"

Healer. (Having felt a reaction and heard a faint 'click') "What happened then?"

Subject "It's off the bone, it's not twisted now and my wrist and hand is throbbing, but not uncomfortably so, a funny feeling really."

Healer. "That's O.K., it will settle down shortly."

Subject. "Yes it's slowing down now, it's becoming more of a gentle pulsing and I've got a slight feeling of pins and needles in my fingers!"

Healer. "What about the colour in the area, is it still brown?"

Subject. "Yes, but it's changing as I look at it. It's becoming red.....no, it's turning pink."

Healer. "Is pink the right colour for it?"

Subject. "Yes... and my wrist and hand both feel much better, the pulsing has stopped and so has the pins and needles feeling."

Healer. "Good, now imagine yourself checking, start in the wrist, then go down into your hand and then into each finger and tell me if you find anything else that needs attention."

Subject. (Following a slight pause). "No, it all looks fine now."

OTHER BODY AND LIMB PAINS

SPRAINS

Sprains can be considered the result of a force or movement that has caused some joint to exceed its normal range of movement capacity. In such cases supporting ligaments can become over-stretched or torn. In some cases fragments of bone attached to the ends of ligaments may be torn off, and possibly with the membrane surrounding the joint also becoming damaged, with blood and bodily fluids seeping into the cavity of the joint. Muscles and tendons may also become torn. Extreme pain, faintness, nausea and shock may be experienced. The joint once having been subjected to strain may become weakened and vulnerable to further strains.

A SPRAIN HEALING METHOD

As a result of the wide variations of possible complications and degrees of effect, in the healing example a severe sprain of a subject's right shoulder is used. However, the same principles apply to all sprains, and except in the more milder cases, following medical attention, such as x-rays.

A SPRAIN HEALING EXAMPLE

The subject reports that he slipped whilst carrying a heavy sack over his shoulder. His doctor has told him it will heal itself, and that he should rest it to help. The subject reports that he is in constant pain, despite the pain relief tablets the doctor has given him, and is being kept awake at night, he now feels exhausted. The subject has had the procedure for healing explained and is now in hypnosis, with the Healer's hands on the subject's shoulder. However, as would be in the case of a sprained arm, wrist or hand, the hand-shaking part of the hypnosis induction procedure has not been used, instead the 'hand passing' has been repeated three times.

Healer. "Now just imagine yourself looking inside your shoulder and then tell me what you imagine yourself looking at."

Subject. "I can only see dark red."

Healer. "What colour should you be seeing for it to feel better?"

Subject. "Pale red or pink."

Healer. "What could you imagine doing to change it to those colours?"

Subject. "I'll imagine a fan blowing cold air into my shoulder."

Healer. Good, keep going and keep me in touch with what's happening."

Subject. "I think it's helping and I keep getting brief images of it looking in a mess in there. I get pictures of swelling and bits broken, but the general area is looking a lighter red."

Healer. "O.K., keep that fan blowing and tell me when the colour has become the correct one."

Subject. "It's still changing, but only slowly, I think I shall have to carry out some repairs before it can change completely."

Healer. "O.K., would it be a good idea to start by repairing some of those broken bits you reported?"

Subject. "Yes, but how can I do that?"

Healer. "You could imagine using a super glue, stitching them back together or imagine replacing them with new parts, or using some other method."

Subject. "I think I'll glue the less damaged bits and replace the others, it will take me a few minutes - there's a lot to be done."

Healer. "Good, keep me in touch with your progress"

Subject. "It's going O.K., and my shoulder feels a bit easier now."

Healer. "Good, then tell me when the repairing and replacing are done."

Subject. "It looks O.K. now, but the muscles are not quite the right colour and look swollen still."

Healer. "How can you reduce the swelling?"

Subject. "I'll imagine massaging in some cream."

Healer. "Good keep me in touch with how it's going."

Subject. "It's working , the muscles seem more relaxed and a nicer colour. It feels odd, when we began it felt hot and painful, now it feels just warm and easier."

Healer. "Good, that's confirmation of the healing taking place."

Note. Particularly in more severe cases, the healing procedure may require further attempts, but at least a gap of four hours between each attempt should be allowed. A similar method to the one given can be applied to any sprained part.

BODILY PAINS

By this it is meant the 'mysterious' pain that seems to defy medical explanation or treatment, and the healing methods should not be attempted until conventional medicine has failed to identify a cause or provided a treatment. For example, only someone marooned on a desert island and with no medical assistant equally marooned with him, should attempt to resolve appendicitis. However, the methods could be used to assist identified causes and treatment.

Bodily pains can also have a variety of causes, such as bad posture, poor nutrition, lack of exercise, over consumption of food - particularly of alcohol, bad diets, rushed eating, over activity - particularly of a repetitive type, and the adverse effects of medication. These are examples of areas worthy of consideration prior to using the method given.
Note. Period pain healing is given under its own heading.

THE BODILY PAIN HEALING METHOD

Following the explanation of his role and with the subject in hypnosis, the method to be followed has much in common with limb healing methods. However, caution should be exercised in the use of laying on of hands, particularly in an opposite sex situation. In such cases either the subjects partner could assist, or failing that, the subject should be asked to lay their own hands on the affected part.

Where the laying on of hands is to be on the back, this cannot easily be done by the subject, and it is more acceptable for the Healer to do so. Since such a wide variety of bodily pains can exist, it is impossible to describe every possibility. However, the subject will be all too aware of their condition and where it is being experienced. The subject is therefore in a good position to explain his condition to the Healer.

A BODILY PAIN HEALING EXAMPLE

The subject has reported that he suffers with a mysterious pain in his right kidney area, and that all medical investigations had failed to indicate a cause, and his doctor has only been able to recommend pain relief medication. The subject has had his role explained to him and is sitting in hypnosis with the Healer holding one hand on the area indicated by the subject.

Healer. "Imagine yourself looking inside this part of your back and have a picture of something come into your mind, and then tell me what you are looking at."

Subject. "I can see a yellow oval blob."

Healer. "Should it be yellow?"

Subject. "No, I don't think so."

Healer. "Then what colour should it be?"

Subject. "Red."

Healer. "How can you imagine changing it to red?"

Subject. "I'm trying to paint it but the paint just runs off."

Healer. "Could you clean it in some way so that the paint can hold?"

Subject. "Yes, I'm trying that but its difficult to clean and its getting hot."

Healer. "Could you use something else that would be more effective and that would cool it too?"

Subject. "Yes, I'll try using some washing up liquid with menthol in it."

Healer. "Good, let me know how it goes."

Subject. "That's it! It's working and its turning brown now."

Healer. "O.K., is brown its right colour to be healthy and well?"

Subject. "No, but now it's brown it's clean, and I can paint it light red."

Healer. "Fine, when its ready paint it light red and let me know when you have."

Subject. "It's coming on well - I've done it and it looks lovely."

Healer. "Look around and tell me if anything else needs fixing."

Subject. "No, it's fixed but its still hurting."

Healer. "Check again, find out why it's still hurting."

Subject. "It's just the healing taking place - I know it - it will be fine soon and I want to stop now."

Healer. "O.K. The healing continues until perfect. Just open your eyes when you're ready then."

Note: Following this, an actual case, and in the way it proceeded, the subject reported significant pain in the area for nearly two hours. Fortunately it then began to ease until completly gone. Despite the previous two years of pain, a year later the subject reported no further discomfort. Although fairly rarely, some temporary side effects can be experienced because a healing change is taking place.

DIABETES

Note. As with many of the conditions occurring throughout this book, it is essential that medical advice be sought. It is particularly important that where a diabetic condition appears to have responded to the healing methods to be described, that regular checks by the subject's doctor be made. These should be at least for a year, and longer where medical advice deems them necessary.

There are two principle forms of diabetes, diabetes insipidus and diabetes mellitus. In both types of diabetes it is sound practice to ask the mind to carry out an examination as a first step.

The questions requiring answering are firstly, has the condition arisen following some psychological impact and, if not, could the condition respond to an attempt to heal.

The psychological factor is found to be common, especially with diabetes mellitus. Where the psychological cause is found to be a factor, the subject could be assisted to resolve this factor.

RESOLVING DIABETES PSYCHOLOGICAL FACTORS

Where a psychological factor is suspected, or has been indicated, this can normally be resolved by using the following method. The subject is relaxed into hypnosis, and following this the Healer is to tell the subject he is going back in his memory to a time that something is happening, or about to happen, that led to his condition emerging. The following is an illustration of the method.

Healer. "Harry you are going back over time, you are recalling and remembering a time when something happened, or was just about to happen that caused your diabetes. Harry, your mind is linking and connecting one thought and memory to another, and you are recalling that memory of what happened to cause your diabetes. I'll count to three, click my fingers, and you have that memory just come to your mid. One, two three 'click'!"

Harry. "I can see me laying on a bed crying."

Healer. "Why are you crying?"

Harry. "Because my mother has been screaming at me."

Healer. "Why has your mother been screaming at you?"

Harry. "Oh yes, I remember now. I've had a row with my wife and gone home to my parents house. There was nobody at home so I broke in. I felt hungry but couldn't be bothered to make myself anything, so I ate a whole box of chocolates that my mother had bought for Christmas."

Healer. "Go into the feelings you had at the time, relive them, feel them."

Harry. (tears emerging) "I was so upset with my wife, now this. I was going

89

to replace the chocolates but my mother just wouldn't listen."

Following this revelation and release, Harry's subconscious was asked if his diabetes could now be released, and replied that it could.

A FURTHER PSYCHOLOGICAL FACTOR EXAMPLE

Following the one, two, three 'click' method, a lady reported that she could see a lemonade bottle. Following this she recalled that during the very hot summer of 1976 she had nearly been run over crossing a road. She had been considerably shocked by the incident. She had returned home and drank a large bottle of lemonade.

This had been taken up by her subconscious as a comfort, causing her to buy two further bottles which she also drank. The shock of the near accident combined with the excessive consumption had disrupted her system and caused her diabetes.

DIABETES INSIPIDUS

In this condition the water balancing function of the body is disturbed, giving rise to considerable thirstiness. The effects of this form of diabetes are due to a deficiency of hormones being released by the pituitary gland, a small pea like part located in the base of the skull. Treatment is usually through hormone replacement.

TREATING DIABETES INSIDIOUS

Following the probe for a psychological factor, the subject is to have his visualisation role explained to him and checked that he understands it. A brief description of his condition is given, and the healing attempt is to be made with the Healer holding his hand on the subject's head, in the area where the neck enters the skull.

A DIABETES INSIPIDUS HEALING EXAMPLE

In much the same way as in previous examples, the subject is to visualise some part requiring attention for healing. In his visualisation the subject is to be encouraged to picture a small gland with a lobe. This lobe is to be investigated to establish why it is failing to produce a sufficient quantity of hormones to stabilise the water-balancing mechanism. The subject may see it as blocked, switched off or only partially working. The gland may be visualised as being short of some nutrient or supply. Valves may need to be opened or 'plumbing' parts need to be replaced.

DIABETES MELLITUS

The more common form of diabetes, and arising within the Pancreas. Basically, in this condition there is a chronic disorder of the digestion and usage of starches and sugars. The condition arises due to a lack of bodily produced insulin, which damages the ability to store and use glucose. Consequently glucose remains in the blood stream, with a loss of sugar in urination. The condition gives rise to increased thirst, urination and a tendency to coma. Treatments include insulin by injection, with a regular and controlled diet - mostly lifelong.

There are special tissues which produce insulin. Insulin is a hormone which controls the metabolism of sugar. In the more severe cases, especially when not treated, the inability to store and use sugars means the body has to derive its energy requirements from other sources, such as from protein and fat. Although diabetes is a disease, no bacterial or viral causes have been detected. Consequently both types lend themselves well to our healing methods.

TREATING DIABETES MELLITUS

In many cases the release of the psychological factor is sufficient by itself to rectify the condition. However, using the healing method to follow can assist in the process. With the subject having been taken into hypnosis, his role understood, the sequence of healing could then proceed as in the following example, preferably with the Healer holding his hand on the subject's pancreas area. (Just above the waistline and to the left of centre of the body.)

A DIABETES MELLITUS A HEALING EXAMPLE

Healer. "Now I want you to imagine yourself to be inside the area I am holding, but looking at where your insulin is produced."

Subject. "I can see some pipes."

Healer. "What do you notice about the pipes, their colours and sizes for example?"

Subject. "They look alright, but I can see one that seems to be sagging down."

Healer. "Why is it sagging?"

Subject. "It's a bit like how a hose pipe sags when it's empty."

Healer. "Imagine feeling it then to see if it's empty."

Subject. "Yes, I think it is empty."

Healer. "Should it be empty?"

Subject. "No, I don't think so."

Healer. "Then start checking to see why it's empty - is some tap or valve closed, or is the pipe caught up or twisted?"

Subject. "It's going to take me some time to do that, there's a lot of pipes and valves down here."

Healer. "O.K., but keep me in touch with what you're doing."

Subject. "I'm having to push the sagging pipe over a bit, so that when it fills up it won't be trapped. Ah, I've done that, and I can see the tap handle that supplies it."

Healer. "Good, is it turned on?"

Subject. "No, and I can't budge it."

Healer. "Could you use some penetrating oil to force it?"

Subject. "No, I'll use a spanner and work it back and forward a little and try to free it that way."

Healer. "O.K., keep me in touch with the progress."

Subject. "It's moving, its getting easier to move it too."

Healer. "Keep going then and let me know what's happening."

Subject. "The pipe is filling and becoming firmer and firmer."

Healer. "Good, go along the pipe to where it leads to and tell me what you find."

Subject. "It leads to a small jet, but nothing's coming out!"

Healer. "Check if the jets are blocked, use a cocktail stick or some other device."

Subject. "UGH! There's a lot of dark wax like sludge coming out."

Healer. "Keep working at it and tell me what happens next."

Subject. "Ah! A squirt of insulin just shot out - it's clearing, it's clearing. The insulin is beginning to come out as a small spray now."

Healer. "Good, is the quality of the insulin good?"

Subject. "I don't know, but there's plenty of it."

Healer. "Can you tell by its colour if it's good quality?"

Subject. "Yes, it's very pale yellow, and that's what it should be."

POOR CIRCULATION

In this condition the general sensation of coldness is reported, but particularly in hands and feet. Females are more prone to this condition than men. One type of poor circulation is known as Raynaud's disease. In this unpleasant condition spasms of the arteries occur, resulting in a paleness of the affected parts and sometimes most of the body, but especially fingers and toes. Good nourishment, exercise, dressing well and avoiding cold conditions can all help, and these should be checked for.

Additionally, the subject should, particularly in more severe cases, be medically examined.

A POOR CIRCULATION TREATMENT METHOD

Taking the subject into hypnosis conduct an enquiry examination to establish if the mind knows of any specific cause for the condition. That is, a psychological or physiological cause. Additionally the subject's

93

subconscious should be asked if, with the Healer's assistance, the circulation could be improved. Even where the subconscious says 'no' to this last question, the healing method should be proceeded with, because in such a case the subconscious may have said 'no' merely believing that to be so. Naturally too, should the subconscious report a psychological factor this should be resolved prior to attempting change.

A POOR CIRCULATION TREATMENT EXAMPLE

The subject, a female, reported that she had such poor circulation, that she had near constant pain in her fingers and toes. To ease this her doctor had suggested that an operation to sever her nerves in toes and fingers would stop the pain. However, there would then be some risk of gangrene resulting in lost digits. Not being inspired by the prospect of this, together with a permanent numbness in her toes and fingers, she visited, asking if she could be helped by our methods. Actually she attended a seminar given to demonstrate the healing methods. Because of the limited time factor a direct approach to healing was decided upon. She was taken into hypnosis and the following was to transpire.

Me. "Subconscious, Mary reports to me that she has a poor circulation problem that causes her great discomfort. Subconscious, shortly I will count to three and click my fingers and you draw Mary's attention to some part of her that causes this condition." (One, two, three click!)

Mary. "Oh! I can see a valentines card with a heart on it."

Me "So is it your heart that needs attention then?"

Mary. "Yes, I think so."

Me. "O.K., imagine yourself looking inside your heart at some point that requires that attention."

Mary. "I'm in a tunnel - it's not very long."

Me. "Good, what colour is it?"

Mary. "A nice pink."

Me. "What else do you notice about it?"

Mary. "It's too small."

94

Me   "How could you make it bigger?"

Mary.   "I don't know."

Me.   "Supposing you were to gently push against the sides with your hands, could that help?"

Mary.   "I'll try.....yes, yes, it's getting wider....I've nearly finished, it's only a short tunnel."

Suddenly there was a gasp from the audience, for instantly she changed colour from ashen grey to bright pink, even through her dark tights her legs could be seen to have changed colour. Mary then reported that she felt hot all over, but feeling more comfortable. One year later Mary reported herself to be fine, and with no circulation problem remaining.

P.M.T. AND PERIOD PAINS

For our healing purposes these conditions may be considered as two variations of the same problem. So common are both that little in the way of describing them is necessary, save that period pains affect the lower part of the females body and the discomfort can even be severe, whilst pre-menstrual tension (P.M.T) affects attitudes and mental reactions. Again, in P.M.T. the results can be severe. In one case for example a woman was excused the charge of murder, having killed her husband during a severe attack.

THE TREATMENT METHOD FOR PERIOD PAINS AND P.M.T.

Commonly both are found to have a similar origin, and that is in an experience linked in some way to the initial menstruation event. As such, in the absence of medical evidence of a detectable cause, both conditions are psychological in origin. In rare cases either condition may occur subsequent to the initial event, but even then it is mostly found to have that psychological factor.

Especially since menstruation commences in most between eleven and thirteen years of age, the memory of the initial event will mostly be readily recalled. However, it is the subconscious reaction to that event that is essential. Therefore the induction of hypnosis and the one, two, three 'click' method are to be employed. Somewhere there is to be found an emotional connection with that first event. Such emotions may stem from not understanding what was happening to her, some adverse reaction to her by her mother, a teacher at school, or someone noticing the signs before she had. There may have been those who frightened her of the forth coming event, or she may have developed her own fears.

Then she may have been the first in her school class, and become emotionally self-conscious, or the last, and had worried that it might not happen to her and she would be the 'odd-one'. So many possibilities exist that the Healer can expect practically anything to be found to have created the condition.

In the period pain we have that negative psychological factor being expressed as discomfort in the bodily area conducting menstruation. In P.M.T. we have the subconscious anxiety with the approaching menstruation. In both cases the subconscious memory of the initial event has become active, as if in this repetition the subconscious is once again reliving the original anxiety.

A PERIOD PAIN AND P.M.T. TREATMENT EXAMPLE

The subject has been taken into hypnosis, and the therapy is to commence.

Healer. "Subconscious, Mary reports to me that she suffers awful discomfort with P.M.T., and then during her period too. Subconscious, Mary wants you to remind her of what happened to cause her discomfort. In a moment I shall count to three, click my fingers and you take Mary back to the time and the memory causing her to suffer as she does. One, two, three click."

Mary "I remember that it started at school, but I just thought I'd wet myself. I asked the teacher if I could leave the class to go to the toilet. She said I couldn't leave, and I became worried because I could feel it still happening. Suddenly I got up and just ran out, with the teacher shouting angrily at me to come back."

Healer. "What happened next?"

Mary "As I ran to the toilet I became afraid of what would happen when I returned to the class, and I began to cry."

Healer. "And what happened then?"

Mary. "When I got to the toilet I found I was in a mess, I tried to clean myself but my panties were so messy I couldn't keep them on anymore."

Healer. "And what did you do then?"

Mary. "I flushed them down the toilet and ran home. I cried all the way and I felt so self conscious and embarrassed."

Healer. "Can you feel those feelings now?"

Mary. "Yes, I feel awful!"

Healer. "Then be there at that time, and go into those feelings deeper still."

Mary. (emotional and crying) "Thank goodness my mother was at home and she was so understanding. The next few days I stayed at home and my mother put matters right with my teacher. I thought I'd got over the experience."

At this point Mary's subconscious was thanked for its help and asked if there was anything else causing her discomfort during menstruation, and it replied 'no'.

Following this her subconscious was asked if the discomfort had now gone and again it replied 'no'. With further questions as to why, her subconscious put a 'one' in her mind. Her subconscious was then asked if this meant one more menstruation needed to occur before the discomfort terminated, and her subconscious said 'yes' to this. Several weeks later Mary said that during the menstruation, which was soon after the therapy, she had only felt minor discomfort, and later she reported to having experienced no further problems.

BROKEN BONE HEALING

In this it is pre-supposed that medical attention has been received, and that the subject either has a need to hasten recovery or to strengthen some bone to prevent further risk.

THE BROKEN BONE TREATMENT METHOD

The subject is to be instructed in the visualisation process to be used and taken into hypnosis. Where possible the Healer is to hold his hand or hands on the area being treated, even if over some plaster cast.

A BROKEN BONE HEALING TREATMENT EXAMPLE

Healer. "Now I want you to imagine that you are looking inside yourself and seeing the bone at the point it needs healing. Tell me what you see."

Subject. "I can imagine it, there's a crack-like line running across it."

Healer. "O.K., how could you fill that crack line so that the bone becomes healed and strong?"

Subject. "I don't know."

Healer. "Could you use some fine rapidly hardening cement?"

Subject. "Yes, very fine - I'm imagining doing it now. Every time I put more on it pushes the last application deeper, so I'll just have to keep going until it's filled."

Healer. "Good, keep working at it until it's filled then."

Subject. "That's got it, I can't force anymore in, it's filled - hey....I can't even see where the cracked line was!"

A BONE STRENGTHENING TREATMENT EXAMPLE

In a similar way given in the broken bone treatment method, the subject is to be taken into hypnosis and had the explanation of his role given to him. Where possible the Healer should use his hands, and hold the area to be treated.

Following this the Healer could continue:

Healer. "I want you to imagine yourself looking at the bone, and tell me what you notice."

Subject. "I'm having difficulty in imagining it all, but I can sense some part and it looks more like old putty in texture."

Healer. "Should it be like that?"

Subject. "Oh no, it should be shining, smooth and hard."

Healer. "How can you make it shinning smooth and hard?"

Subject. "I could scrape the putty stuff off with the edge of a nail file."

Healer. "O.K., see yourself doing that and keep me informed of your progress."

Subject. "It's coming off easily but the bone underneath looks pitted and dull."

Healer. "Let me know when all the putty stuff is off."

Subject. "I think that's got it, I'll just dust it off."

Healer. "When that's finished what could you do to make the bone shining smooth and hard?"

Subject. "I've finished cleaning the putty stuff off, but I don't know how to make the bone hard and shiny."

Healer. "Suppose you gently poured some liquid calcium over the bone, so that it would soak in until the bone became solid as it dried."

Subject. "Yes I'll do that, I've seen something like that done before some where. I'm starting now at the top and working down. The bone just keeps soaking it up, like water on sand."

Healer. "Keep going, it will fill soon."

Subject. "It's taking some time, but the liquid calcium is not sinking in as fast, so it must be filling up now."

Healer. "Good tell me when no more will soak in."

Subject. "That's it, it was just flowing off so I've stopped pouring it on."

Healer. "What do you need to do next?"

Subject. "I'm watching it turning hard and shiny, it looks smooth too."

Healer. "When it's hard I want you to imagine trying to scratch it with your nail, and tell me what happens."

Subject. "Nothing, it is too hard to be scratched now."

PART SIX

STROKES & CANCERS

STROKES

There are four principal causes of a stroke:

(a) Blood leakage from an artery. (Cerebral Haemorrhage).
(b) A blood clot in an artery. (Cerebral Thrombosis).
(c) The blockage and artery by fats, bacterial mass or an air bubble. (Cerebral Embolism).
(d) Pressure on a blood vessel by a tumour. High blood pressure and arteriosclerosis among others can also play a part, as can shock, stress and violent exertion. In the treatment methods to follow the holding of hands on the subject's head, or just above it is recommended.

TREATING CEREBRAL HAEMORRHAGE

In hypnosis the subject is asked to imagine that he is looking down on his brain, rather as he might view a cauliflower in a container with the lid off. He is to report any area of discoloration, and then be asked to imagine himself cleansing that area in some way. Having done that, the next step is for the subject to imagine himself identifying the blood vessel that bled, and the point at which it did. This point located is to be imagined as being repaired and re-inforced in some way.

Following this, the subject is to imagine himself checking his entire cerebral blood circulation system, and further re-enforcing either areas requiring strengthening or even the entire network. Following this, where some physical disability has occurred, the subject should be encouraged to visualising himself conducting some physical activities as he previously did. The subject then, and still in hypnosis, is to be further encouraged to participate in the physical exercises described below.

PHYSICAL EXERCISES FOR
STROKE CONDITIONS

In hypnosis, preferably with eyes closed to aid concentration, the Healer, having explained to the subject what is to take place, is seeking to strengthen and improve the bodily parts effected. For example, a weakened hand or arm, leg or foot, impairment of an area of the body. In the case of an arm or hand, for instance, the Healer is to place the palm of his hand on the palm of the subjects hand. Having done so the subject is then asked to begin movements, by turning his hand or pushing, which the Healer is to offer gentle resistance to.

This activity is to take three minutes or so on each occasion the therapy is applied, with several such exercises being conducted at each session, but not in a way that may overtax the subject. In exactly the same way the leg and foot are to be exercised as with the hand and arm.

Where bodily parts are affected the subject is to be encouraged to make movement exercises in the given area, but this time either unaided by the Healer, or by the Healer holding the subject's hands and gently assisting with the movements taking place. In all of this a suggestion to the subject's subconscious that the subject is improving or doing well, can provide a powerful psychological boost.

A CEREBRAL HAEMORRHAGE
TREATMENT EXAMPLE

The subject has a weak right arm and hand, and has difficulty in walking. The subject is in hypnosis and has had his role explained to him as given in the Treating Cerebral Haemorrhage example.

Healer. "Peter, I want you to imagine that you are looking down at your brain, as if it were a cauliflower inside some container with the lid off, and tell me if you can imagine some part that requires attention, such as some stained or discoloured part."

Peter. "I think I can see a brownish patch where the stroke occurred."

Healer. "What colour should it be?"

Peter. "I think it should all be a creamy grey."

Healer. "Then how can you turn it to creamy grey?"

Peter.   "I'll rinse it gently by applying a fine spray and dissolve the brown away. It's coming on nicely.....yes, it looks clean now, just like the rest."

Healer.   "Excellent, now imagine yourself exploring the blood vessel which caused the problem, and look for the point where the blood seeped out."

Peter.   "Yes, I've got it I think, and it looks as if it's got a small crack that has began to join together, like a sore cut on a finger."

Healer.   "What can you do to re-enforce the healing?"

Peter.   "I'll stitch it like they do with cuts."

Healer.   "O.K., tell me when you have."

Peter.   "That's done - it looks fine."

Healer.   "Good, now imagine yourself checking the entire blood circulation system in your head, looking for any other areas which might need re-enforcing or some other attention."

Peter.   "It will take time, there's a lot to be checked."

Healer.   "That's OK., there's no hurry but let me know what you find."

Peter.   "It looks a bit dodgy down there, the pipes are too thin."

Healer.   "How could you strengthen them?"

Peter.   "I'm imagining some nutrient in the blood flushing through them, soaking into the walls and making them thicker and stronger, yes, much stronger."

Healer.   "Tell me when you've completed that."

Peter.   "It's done, it all looks cleaner and better than before."

Visualising himself conducting some physical activities as he formerly did, and after this, the physical exercises described are to follow.

Note. Several repetitions of the visual and physical exercises may be required.

TREATING CEREBRAL THROMBOSIS

In hypnosis the subject is asked to imagine himself locating the blocked blood vessel, as if it were a tube that had become blocked. Seeing himself flushing the head's circulation system with a dissolving substance is best in this instance, rather than implying some imagination of the blockage moving - to goodness knows where. Additionally some nutrient might be imagined as being circulated in the blood system to prevent any re-occurrence.

A CEREBRAL THROMBOSIS TREATMENT EXAMPLE

The subject is in hypnosis, and has had his role explained to him in the manner set out in the, 'Treating Cerebral Thrombosis' example.

Healer. "I want you to imagine that you are looking at the point in the blood vessel that has caused the problem."

Betty. "I'm imagining myself looking at a red pipe - it's swollen a bit."

Healer. "O.K., what's causing that swelling, go inside the pipe and examine it there."

Betty. "It looks like a piece of purple jelly that's got lodged."

Healer. "How can you dissolve it away?"

Betty. "I don't know, shall I squeeze it so it floats away?"

Healer. "I think I may have some ideas myself that could solve it. Supposing that, just like you can with jelly, you were to warm it and watch it melt, or, even better perhaps, imagine some natural solvent coming through the blood to dissolve it?"

Betty. "I can see it melting, just like the jelly lumps do when you pour hot water on them, it's dissolving away and the pipes shrinking back to normal, and I can actually feel a change taking place in my head,"

Healer. "Good, the head is feeling the relief of the problem taking place, but keep your eye on that jelly bit until it's dissolved completely, and tell me when it has."

Betty.   "It's gone, melted away completely and my head actually feels better."

Healer. "Good, Betty, would it also be a good idea to imagine some nutritional solvent to be increased in the blood supply to make it impossible for any other jelly lumps to form?"

Betty.   "Well yes, but how do I do that?"

Healer. "Imagine yourself finding the tap or valve supply outlet and turning the supply on further."

Betty.   "That's the cause of the problem, it's barely on. And it's stiff, but it's turning and there's plenty of it now."

Where applicable, the visualisation and physical exercises should next be undertaken.

TREATING TUMOUR INDUCED STROKES

In this the tumour itself is the main objective of the treatment method, with the blood supply then being visualised as returning to normal with the release of the pressure on the affected blood vessel. Where applicable the visualisation of a return to normal physical abilities and the physical exercises are to be incorporated following the initial treatment.

In the treatment of tumour induced strokes the tumour is to be visualised. Following this, some method of reducing it, removing it or confining it should be used. Among such methods the subject might simply see it shrinking, melting away, hungry birds pecking at it like they do with seeds, and literally eating it away. A further idea, the subject may imagine dissolving it, isolating it from its nutritional source so that it just fades away, operating on it, gradually slicing it away, imagine himself able to blow it away and then seeing it gone, or peeling it like an onion until it has been eliminated.

Such ideas are to be put to the subject, who may use one or more in combination. Repeated sessions may be called for, indeed be expected.

A TUMOUR INDUCED STROKE
TREATMENT EXAMPLE

Having had his role explained to him and in hypnosis, the subject is to imagine he can see the tumour.

Healer. "What does it look like?"

Subject. "Like a small grey marble."

Healer. "What can you do to get rid of it then?"

Subject. "Well it's not hard like a marble, it's like a small grey rubber ball."

Healer. "O.K., how can you get rid of that small rubber ball then?"

Subject. "No, it's not a ball, it's more like half a ball sticking out and pushing against the vein."

Healer. "So what can you do to release the pressure on the vein?"

Subject. "I'm going to try pricking it, like you might a blister."

Healer. "O.K., tell me what happens when you have."

Subject. "Nothing, it's not made of fluid in there, I need to try something else."

Healer. "What comes to mind?"

Subject "Let me think about it - Ah yes, I'm going to make a slit under it at the base and pump in some silicone, like they do to stop damp rising in walls, that will cut off it's supplies so that it can no longer grown any bigger. I'm doing that now, and there's no blood or any thing leaking out."

Healer. "Good, tell me when you've done that."

Subject. "Yes, I've done that. Now I'm going to start trimming it back with a scalpel, like you might trim a corn."

Healer. "O.K., keep me in touch with your progress."

Subject. "Yes it's just like the texture of a corn, but a bit softer. The vein is filling out too as the thing becomes thinner."

Healer. "Good, let me know when you've trimmed it all off down to silicone level."

Subject. "That's it, I could feel the blade grate on the silicone."

105

CANCER

Cancer may be defined as the unregulated growth of new cells which lack the useful function of their parent tissue, and serving no useful function. Cancer can remain localised in or on the body, or can spread. Despite substantial research little is known as to why cells should act in this way.

Names are given for cancer conditions, such as leukaemia, the proliferation of malignant blood cells. However, including blood cancer there are three types relating to the cells affected. Skin cancer, which is cancer of the cells covering the outer body and lining internal passages and closed cavities, and in malignant cancer is known as carcinoma. Cancer in other bodily cells is referred to as sarcoma. For our treatment methods however, the technicalities of cancer may be largely ignored, leaving us more concerned as to where the cancer is and attempting to heal the condition instead.

Indeed, I have even been successful in treating a cancerous condition without knowing it's type or location. In all cases a psychological factor should be explored for, and this will often be found. Naturally any psychological factor has to be resolved prior to healing attempts. In fact many cases are encountered where the psychological factor is the sole cause, and in treating it the condition can even be illuminated by that method alone. Especially where the condition's onset has followed some highly emotional event, such as the demise of a loved one as an example.

TREATING CANCER CONDITIONS

In hypnosis the psychological factor is first sought and released where it is found to exist. Following such a release the treatment method is similar to that given for brain tumours, set out in the treatment of strokes, where a tumour has been the causual factor. Where possible the laying on of a hand or hands would be used during the therapy.

A CANCER TREATMENT EXAMPLE

In this actual case, a lady attended having been told by her consultant that she could only expect to live for no more than two more months; her five year long battle with her cancer having been lost. Following the induction of hypnosis it was decided to probe for the psychological factor by speaking directly with her subconscious. The ladies subconscious responded well to the approach, which proceeded as follows.

Healer.   "Subconscious, Ann reports to me that she is dreadfully upset because for five years she has suffered with cancer which is threatening her life. Subconscious, you have always looked after Ann and she desperately needs your help now. Subconscious, shortly I will ask you some questions, and when I do, here's how you respond. Subconscious, you take control of Ann's vocal cords and cause her to answer those questions. Subconscious, have you caused Ann's cancer to come into being?"

Ann.   "Yes."

Healer. "Then, if you thought it appropriate, could you cause her cancer to go into remission, totally completely and permanently?"

Ann.   "Yes."

Healer. "Then why have you caused Ann's cancer to come into being?"

Ann.   (Shouting the reply) "Because Ann's nasty, big headed and deserves to die!"

Healer. "Subconscious, if I where to put forward a better idea for taking care of Ann, would you be prepared to consider it?"

Ann.   "Yes."

Healer. "Subconscious, it will take me some time to get to know Ann before I can put that idea forward. Would you grant me that time by sending her cancer into remission now?"

Ann.   "Yes."

Healer. "Then I'll count to three, click my fingers and you do what you need to create that remission. One two three 'click'."

Ann.   (Suddenly opening her eyes) "My God, it was as if an electric shock ran through my entire body."

During the analysis, which took six weeks to complete, Ann was to reveal the extensive negative thoughts she had had about herself for many years. She had literally condemned herself to death as a punishment, which, acting on that instruction, her subconscious had responded to with her cancer. A point of major interest is that it was never asked, nor volunteered by Ann, where the cancer was located or what form it took. More than six months later Ann was contacted, she was well, had gone back to work, was getting on with a normal life, and reported that she was far happier than she had ever felt before.

Note: In the above case no attempt at dealing directly with her cancer was made. Having listened to her during analysis and having allowed herself to formulate a far more positive view of herself, the idea promised earlier to her subconscious was put forward and enthusiastically accepted, as follows.

Me. Subconscious, Ann reports to me that she now feels much happier about herself and realises she had previously misjudged her true value. Subconscious, when we first met I asked if you would be prepared to consider a better idea for looking after her and you said you would. Now I know Ann, and she feels so much happier about herself, my idea is that you love Ann, take care of her, look after her and compensate her for the anxiety she suffered in the past by giving her a fulfilling and satisfying life. Subconscious, would you agree that idea would be better for Ann?"

Ann. "Yes, yes."

Healer. "Then I'll count to three, click my fingers and you incorporate that idea as your principal objective. One, two three 'click'.

A SECOND CANCER TREATMENT EXAMPLE

In this example no psychological factor has been revealed, and the immediate and direct attempt at healing has been decided upon. Brian is shortly due for an operation but wants to try to help himself meanwhile. Brian understands his role of visualisation and imagination, and is in hypnosis ready to begin the treatment of his bladder cancer. Brian has his own hands held on the area.

Healer. "I want you to imagine that you are inside your bladder and looking around at it and tell me what you imagine yourself seeing."

Brian. "Nothing, it's just black."

Healer. "Then imagine there's a light you can switch on, or that you have a torch you can use."

Brian. "I've switched the light on, I'm looking at something like a wide well, but it's got blood in the water."

Healer. "O.K., but how did the blood get into the water, look around the bladder to find out."

Brian.   "Ugh! Part of the well's wall is pushing in, it seems bloated, dark red, messy and seeping blood."

Healer   "So what can you do to heal that area.?"

Brian   "I'm not sure, it needs a lot doing to it though."

Healer. "Imagine yourself examining that bloated area, by touching it perhaps, and tell me if that suggests a way of healing it."

Brian.   "Yes, it's soft to the touch, I could try using a potato peeler on it and peel it away."

Healer. "O.K., keep me in touch with your progress."

Brian.   "It's not peeling like potatoes do, it's just coming away instead."

Healer. "O.K., keep going until you reach healthy tissue."

Brian.   (Following two minutes silence and displaying facial expressions representing his efforts). "Ah! - I've done it, I've got back to the healthy tissue."

Healer. "What do you need to do next?"

Brian.   "I need to go to the toilet, I'm bursting."

Brian visits the toilet and returns looking concerned. He reports that his urine is heavily discoloured, but concluded this must be the result of the healing, which he wishes to continue with. Brian is again taken into hypnosis, and the treatment recommenced.

Healer. "O.K. Brian, go back into your bladder and tell me what you see there now."

Brian.   "The well seems nearly empty, but there's a lot of sludge at the bottom,"

Healer. "And what about the area you were working on?"

Brian.   "It looks a bit sore now, and there's still a little blood left on the surface."

Healer. "O.K. what should you do next?"

Brian.   "I'll gently sponge it down, that will clean it and ease it, like you do with a graze. I've done that. Now I'm going to coat it with a magical cream that will seal the surface from becoming bloated again."

Healer. "Good, let me know when it's done."

Brian.   "That's it! It looks good now."

Healer. "Now what should you do to get rid of the sludge you mentioned?"

Brian.   "I'm hosing it away down the drain."

Healer. "Good, Tell me when you've finished that."

Brian.   "Yes, that's it - it looks nice and clean there now."

Note: This approach may require repeating.

A THIRD CANCER TREATMENT EXAMPLE

In this example the powerful effects of suggestion therapy is to be incorporated. Sue is in hypnosis, has had her role explained, and has found no psychological factor to account for her condition. (The location of which is immaterial for this example). The suggestion is given with positive emotion.

Healer. "Sue, your subconscious has loved you and looked after you all your life. Your subconscious is totally dedicated to your well being and good health. Sue, your subconscious knows exactly how to help you become perfectly fit and healthy. Right now, because of this, your subconscious is doing everything necessary to restore you to perfect health and totally, absolutely and permanently free from your condition."

Healer. (Continuing) Your subconscious is healing, mending and repairing, your subconscious is enthusiastically determined to restore you to perfect health. Your subconscious is restoring your health because it wants to, because it's logical, because it's easy to do, because it makes you so much happier, healthier and fitter.

(This statement should be repeated by introducing the repetition by saying. "Sue, I'm going to pass this important message to your subconscious again.").

Healer. (Continuing) "Sue, I want you to imagine you're looking inside that area, so that you can help your subconscious restore your health in the way it has now started. Let me know what you imagine yourself seeing."

Sue.   "It's a red swelling."

Healer. "Then what can you imagine yourself doing to reduce this swelling until it's gone?"

Sue.   "I could try looking at it, and using my determination make it go away, I could imagine it just shrinking away."

Healer. "Good it is going away, it is shrinking , just as your subconscious is making that happen. Sue, just watch as your subconscious works to reduce it, like a small balloon going down. Now keep telling me what happens."

Sue.   "Yes, it's flattening and flattening."

Healer. "That's because both you and your subconscious are healing it away. It's going Sue, it's going."

Sue.   "I can hardly see it, it's looking almost normal."

Healer. "Tell me when it's completly normal then."

Sue.   "Yes, it looks better now, but like that balloon you mentioned it looks a bit wrinkled."

Healer. "O.K., you can get rid of those wrinkles, perhaps by brushing or scraping them off."

Sue.   "No - their going away too, just like small wrinkles do when your ironing."

Healer. "Good, now I want you to help your subconscious illuminate anything that caused the condition."

Sue.   "What shall I do to do that?"

Healer. "You could take a firm brush and brush off all the cells on the surface that were faulty and reproduced other faulty cells."

Sue.   "Yes, I'm doing that and those cells are coming away easily, just like little pink dots - OH! They turn white as they leave - they are dead cells now."

Healer. "Good. Sue, your subconscious is delighted with the restoration of your good healthy fitness. For your part you are amazed at how quickly you got better, you take enormous satisfaction and pride in your good health which is now returning rapidly and completely."

Note: This therapy can be repeated.

PART SEVEN

FURTHER HEALING METHODS

SURGERY AND ACCIDENT RECOVERY

So many variations and types of surgery and accidents can occur, and with the limitless permutations of bodily locations and their degree of seriousness or severity, that it would be impracticable to cover all contingencies.

THE TREATMENT METHODS FOR SURGERY AND ACCIDENT RECOVERY

In both cases any psychological shock factor should be probed for and resolved prior to the healing attempt, which is basically aimed at improving or speeding recovery.

In the treatment of these conditions the subject is to have his imagination and visualisation role explained to him, with the treatment carried out in hypnosis. Where appropriate the laying on of hands, or hands being held close to the area being treated is to be employed.

Additionally, health restorative suggestions may be made to the subject's subconscious. Such suggestions could included: "(Subject's name), you are returning to perfect health, your subconscious is restoring you, making you fit and well." "(Subject's name), your subconscious takes enormous pride and pleasure in your rapid recovery which is already taking place." "Right now your subconscious is doing everything it needs too to restore you to perfect fitness." Health restorative suggestions should be given prior to treatment and to follow it.

In the examples to follow, both serve to illustrate methods which could equally apply to other cases.

AN ACCIDENT TREATMENT EXAMPLE

Ian fell whilst painting his house. His ladder had slipped as he had stretched out further than he should have. He first fell on the edge of his garage's flat roof, breaking two ribs and cutting his face as he did. He had then fallen on a pile of bricks, breaking his ankle, before rolling to the ground and biting his tongue as he did so. He had immediately been taken to hospital where he had been treated. Now several days later, Ian reports that he remains in pain, is stiff and still swollen. The combination of his ankle fracture and his ribs makes it difficult for him to move.

Ian has been told that two to three repeated sessions of treatment may need to be conducted, each two or three days apart. His role has been explained to him and he has been induced into hypnosis.

Healer. "Ian, what part do you want to work on first?"

Ian. "My ribs, it's the main problem and the most painful, it hurts when I breathe and the Doctor at the hospital said I'd punctured my lung."

Healer. "O.K. then, shall we first look at the ribs, say the top one first, and at the point of the fracture."

Ian. "I can see it, it's like a cup handle that's been broken and stuck together again, but it's not stuck very well, there's still a wide crack."

Healer. "Right, then how could you fill that crack and make the join strong?"

Ian. "I could fill it with a strong glue like Araldite."

Healer. "O.K., do that and tell me when you have."

Ian. "Yes, that's fine, I've used rapid setting Araldite and it's hardening nicely."

Healer. "Now go down to the next rib and look at the fracture there."

Ian. "It's the same as the first one, and I'm applying the glue to that one. That's it, it looks good too."

Healer. "Good, what about the tissue in that area, have a look at it."

114

Ian.   "It's dark red and swollen."

Healer.   "What could you do to reduce the swelling?"

Ian.   "I could try gently massaging some cool soothing ointment into it."

Healer.   "O.K., do that and tell me how it goes."

Ian   "The swelling is going down and the tissue is becoming pinker, so I'll keep going and tell you when it's finished. That's it, - Good grief! I actually feel easier too!"

Healer.   "Excellent, now look at the lung where it was punctured and tell me what you imagine seeing."

Ian.   "I can see two small splits, they are healing up but they could do with some help."

Healer.   "What could you do to help?"

Ian.   "Stitch them?"

Healer.   "Try that, draw the stitches so that they produce invisible mends."

Ian.   "I can feel a sensation in my lung - it's a bit odd but O.K."

Healer.   "That's the healing taking place, look at the lung you have worked on and tell me what you see now."

Ian.   "I can't find the holes - no, wait, I think I can see one, but only just, it's going to be O.K."

Healer.   "Good, would you like to try a deep breath and tell me how it feels?"

Ian.   "Yes, that's much better. Thank you."

Healer.   "What should we work on next?"

Ian.   "What about the ankle?"

Healer.   (Informing Ian of my intention to hold his ankle.) "O.K. then, go down there and tell me what you find."

Ian.   "I can see a white bone that is cracked and chipped."

Healer.   "Would it be a good idea to fix that crack and then fill in the chipped areas afterwards?"

Ian.   "Yes, I could do that using the glue again. It will take a lot more glue though because it's a thicker bone."

Healer.   "O.K., start the gluing and keep me in touch with your progress."

Ian.   "It's coming on, it's coming on..... Ah! It's done and setting."

Healer.   "Good, tell me when it's set."

Ian.   "It's set, and I'm building up the chipped areas now."

Healer.   "Let me know when you've completed that too."

Ian.   "That's fine, I've done it."

Healer.   "What about the tissues in that area, the muscles and tendons for example?"

Ian.   "The tendons look O.K., but the muscle is swollen."

Healer.   "How could you reduce that swelling?"

Ian.   "Ah! I could rub some ice crystals into it."

Healer.   "Good, do that and tell me what happens."

Ian.   "My ankle actually feels coldish, but the swelling is going down nicely."

Healer.   "What shall we tackle next?"

Ian.   "My face, I'm very self conscious of the bruising, and it's very tender too."

Healer.   O.K., imagine yourself inside your face in that area, look around it and tell me what you see."

Ian.   "It's a mess, it's swollen and discoloured with the bruising."

Healer. "How could you get rid of the swelling?"

Ian. "It's the blood leaked into the area, but I don't know how to remove it."

Healer. "Could you imagine washing it away, perhaps using a hosepipe like you do to clean a path or patio?"

Ian. "Yes I'll try that... it's like the mud and bits you wash off a path, but this is the leaked blood being washed away."

Healer. "Good, tell me when it's cleaned up."

Ian. "I can imagine it cleaned up, but I know it's still there."

Healer. "That's O.K. because your subconscious it clearing the area now, but it could take it a little while to complete the task. Try feeling your face, and tell me if you notice any difference."

Ian. "Yes, I think it feels more comfortable."

Healer. "Good, it will improve quite quickly now, but it will probably need a little longer."

Ian. "Yes, I understand that - could we do something about my swollen tongue now? I still can't eat solids."

Healer. "Right, then go inside your tongue and see what's causing the swelling."

Ian. "I'm looking at it from above, and can see it all swollen. What should I try here?"

Healer. "Could you try just watching it shrinking back to normal?"

Ian. "Yes, but it needs something to cause that to happen."

Healer. "Well we used ice in the ankle and that worked well. So could you try imagining yourself sucking a smooth disc of ice?"

Ian. "Yes, that could do it... it's there, lovely, cool and refreshing too."

Healer. "Look at your tongue now Ian and tell me what you notice."

Ian.   "It's going down slowly and it actually feels smaller. It will take several ice discs though."

A SURGERY TREATMENT EXAMPLE

Jan has recently had a hysterectomy and wishes to try to speed her recovery. She has had her role explained to her and been induced into hypnosis. Jan is sitting with her right hand on the area of the area of the operation.

Healer.   "Jan, imagine your inside where you're holding your hand, look around you and tell me what you're drawn to."

Jan.   "I can see lots of red down here, it looks sore and I think the parts that were cut in the surgery have not healed yet."

Healer.   "So what do you feel you could do to help with your recovery?"

Jan.   "I think it needs cleaning first."

Healer.   "How can you imagine yourself doing that?"

Jan.   "Should I try using some small cotton wool buds moistened in clean water?"

Healer.   "That seems a good idea, try that."

Jan.   "I'm imagining some of those flour graders doing it for me, they seem happy to help, and there're putting the used cotton buds in a kitchen waste bin."

Healer.   "Tell me the effect that those flour graders are having."

Jan.   "I can imagine them humming as they work, and it's getting a pinker sort of colour."

Healer.   "Tell me when it's all pinker."

Jan.   "It's nearly there, but it's taking time to clean the little corners and deeper parts."

Healer.   "Watch them keep trying, they will soon have it cleaned."

Jan.   "Yes, it looks almost done."

Healer. "While they complete the cleaning, could you help with some other healing?"

Jan.   "Yes, what should I do?"

Healer. "Could you work on the area where the surgery was done?"

Jan.   "Yes, alright, I think I need to seal them somehow, and I'm trying to think how."

Healer. "What about using some clear cream from a tube that you can squeeze?"

Jan.   "Yes, O.K., I'm running it around all the edges."

Healer. "How do those edges look as you seal them?"

Jan.   "Nice, and they've stopped looking sore and inflamed too."

Healer. "Let me know when it's all done."

Jan.   "I think that's it, and the flour graders have done a good job too, it's all looking much better now."

Healer. "What do you need to do next?"

Jan.   "It looks sort of weak from the operation now I come to think of it, but the heat from my hand is making it feel better."

Healer. "How could you help to make it stronger in there?"

Jan.   "Should I try flushing it with a strengthening solution?"

Healer. "Yes, try that and tell me what you imagine happening."

Jan.   "It's looking stronger and feels much better now."

Note. In most cases the therapy will require repetition.

THE TREATMENT METHODS
FOR MORE MINOR CONDITIONS

In treating minor conditions, such as a small cut, a slight sprain, a burn, a graze, a hurt finger or 'knock', the induction of hypnosis can mostly be unnecessary, nor too does the subject need to have his role explained to him. Indeed, no words need even be used, and only the physical actions of the Healer may need to be enacted. However, of course, in the more serious cases, hypnosis, role explanations and a dialogue between Healer and subject do need to be incorporated.

MINOR CONDITION HEALING EXAMPLES

The subject reports a mysteriously stiff finger part which she indicates. She says that she has only been aware of it since the day before. The Healer asks her to hold her hand out flat at the height of her elbow. Following this the Healer then holds her hand in a sandwich like fashion, ensuring his palms are above and below the finger to be healed. This posture being held for about one minute results in tiny internal movements being felt by each in that finger area. To her amazement the finger part returns to normal.

In a second event, a neighbour, on moving in, was seen to be wearing a bandage on his wrist, this had not been there when he had first arrived. On enquiry the new neighbour reported that he had sprained his wrist moving a heavy box. The neighbour was asked to hold his arm out through the open bay window.

By holding both hands, one on each side of his wrist, and not quite touching it, the new neighbour became amazed to find that his wrist rapidly changed to normal and the sprain 'mysteriously' disappeared. Half-an-hour later the new neighbour was seen waiving the removal men farewell as they left, minus his bandage which he had removed as unnecessary.

SCLEROSIS

In this condition there is a hardening of tissue. This may have been caused by inflammation, a restricted blood supply or toxaemia-poisoning. Any tissue or area can be effected. The more common examples are cerebral sclerosis, in which a reduced blood supply to the brain causes damage to the nerves, arteriosclerosis, in this condition the blood vessels become hardened and inelastic, and sclerosis of the liver, where the function of the liver becomes reduced by blockages. However, this last condition is referred to as cirrhosis.

A SCLEROSIS TREATMENT METHOD

The approaches to be made to these conditions are three fold.

Firstly. That the subject avoids any further exposure to contributing causes, such as in cirrhosis of the liver, where excessive alcohol has been responsible. In most cases the subject will have received advice from his doctor, if he has not, such advice should be sought. Knowing the contributing cause, such as in cirrhosis of the liver brought on by excessive alcohol consumption, the information may call for the Healer to reinforce a change in habit or mental attitude.

Secondly. In each case using mind imagery, the affected parts are to be 'flushed' or 'cleaned'.

Thirdly. The area, is to be rejuvenated, particularly with blood vessels, by applying some form of enhancer during the visualisation and imagery part of the therapy. Holding a hand or hands on the area during therapy can considerably enhance the treatment. Since the approach to cerebral sclerosis has much in common with arteriosclerosis, this and cirrhosis of the liver are the two chosen for examples.

AN ARTERIOSCLEROSIS TREATMENT EXAMPLE

Roger has had his painful leg condition diagnosed as arteriosclerosis. He has received medical advice and treatment. With his leg still painful, and fearful that his doctor had told him that should the condition deteriorate that at some point amputation would have to be considered, he has attended to attempt Mind Over Matter Self-Healing. Roger has had his visualisation and imagination role explained to him, and is in hypnosis with the Healer holding his hands on Roger's right thigh.

Healer. "I want you to imagine yourself looking into your leg in the area I'm holding, and find yourself drawn to some part and tell me what you see."

Roger. "I think I can see a dark red tube or pipe."

Healer. "Should it be dark red?"

Roger. "I don't think so, it looks a bit swollen too."

121

Healer. "What can you imagine yourself doing, what would make it a better colour and reduce the swelling too?"

Roger. "It's dark red and swollen because it's congested, it needs flushing."

Healer. "O.K., how can you flush it?"

Roger. "I think I'll turn on a tap that makes a thinning substance flow through the pipe."

Healer. "O.K. then, do that and keep me in touch with what happens."

Roger. "I've turned on a red tap with a round circular top, and the thinner is flowing through. I can imagine a lot of fatty stuff on the pipe's lining but it's beginning to melt slowly and its making the whole of my leg feel tingly and warmer, especially where your holding your hands."

Healer. "Good, that's the healing taking place. Keep looking at that pipe and let me know how it goes."

Roger. "It's taking a little while because it's a long pipe. Will you move your hands down a few inches as we continue?"

Healer. "O.K., I'll do that."

Roger. "That's fine, my whole leg feels much warmer, and that fatty stuff is still melting away. I see it more like ice crystals in a pipe with warm water flowing through it now."

Healer. "Good, how's the pipe looking from the outside now?"

Roger. "It's turning a paler red now, and it looks thinner too."

Healer. "Good, I'll move my hands further down now, keep me posted on your progress."

Roger. "The whole leg seems far more comfortable now, and I feel the relief in my body too"

Healer. "Good, that's the release of the circulation becoming generally better. Now imagine seeing into the pipe again and tell me what

122

you notice now."

Roger. "I can feel a lot of small movements up and down the leg, but inside it, have you felt them with your hands?"

Healer. "Yes I have, and that's good, it's part of the healing. Now look inside that pipe now and tell me what it looks like."

Roger. "I'm travelling through it, it looks much cleaner, but let me complete my inspection of the whole length."

Healer. "Please carry on, and let me know the result of your inspection."

Roger. (A little later) "Yes, I've done that, it's so much better already, but I need to leave the tap on so that the thinner can keep flowing to finish the job and keep the pipe free."

Healer "Right, now would it be a good idea to reinforce our work by rejuvenating that pipe, so that it becomes more flexible and much fitter?"

Roger. "Well yes, but how can I do that?"

Healer. "How about turning on another tap that supplies a sort of thin cream that will soak into the pipe wall making it pliable and flexible?"

Roger. "Yes, I'll do that. I can see the tap, it's green and I'm turning it on now, it is flowing well and just as you said, it's making the pipe far more supple and flexible.

Healer "O.K., and how does the pipe look from the outside now?"

Roger. "Much better, it's not swollen and it's more normal in size."

Note. This treatment may need to be repeated. Where it is preferred the hands may be held a little away from the part being treated, and in such a case should be moved down from the top area of the leg in stages, until the foot has also been treated.

A CIRRHOSIS OF THE LIVER TREATMENT EXAMPLE

Barry has been diagnosed as having this condition, and is receiving medical treatment. Barry originally attended for assistance to give up his remaining temptation to continue with his heavy drinking. Following this he has asked for assistance to speed his recovery. Barry's role has been explained to him and he has been relaxed into hypnosis. The Healer has his right hand resting on the area in front of Barry's liver.

Healer.   "Barry, I want you to imagine you are looking down here and inside at your liver and then tell me what you see."

Barry.   "It's dark down there but I can see something, it's large - very dark brown-red, but it has some whitish marks."

Healer   "Fine, are those the correct colours for it to be healthy and fit for it's role?"

Barry.   "No, I don't think so - the dark brown red seems O.K., but not that grey-white speckled colouring."

Healer.   "Then why is it speckled grey-white?"

Barry.   "It's a bit like a sponge, and the grey-white speckles are blockages in it. - Rather like wax - no, it's not wax it's more like some fatty stuff."

Healer.   "Those fatty blockages, how could you remove them?"

Barry.   "There's so many I can't pick them out, anyway I couldn't imagine picking fat out because it's too soft."

Healer.   "So what about some other method then, like flushing it with a dissolving liquid, perhaps as washing up liquid would do with a fatty blocked sponge?"

Barry.   "Yes, that's what I'm doing. I'm dipping it in warm water with washing up liquid in it....the fatty stuff is coming out as I squeeze it and then let go."

Healer.   "Good, keep going and keep me informed on your progress."

Barry.   "It will take several attempts and I shall need to change the water soon."

Healer.   "Good, keep doing that, changing the water and soap mix as you need to."

Barry.   (A little later) "It seems fine now, the holes are clear and it seems nice and spongy too."

Healer. "Excellent, what do you need to do next"

Barry.   "I'm not sure, it looks pretty good as it is."

Healer. "What I have in mind is to rejuvenate it in some way. What I am thinking of is to put something back that will help it to become not just clean but fitter."

Barry.   "What do you suggest then?"

Healer. "Well, what about some healthy restorative nutrient mixture that restores your liver to perfect health and efficiency?"

Barry.   "Yes, I see that, the liver needs feeding as well as cleaning, the fatty stuff has been preventing those nutrients from feeding my liver with what it needs to do it's job. How do you suggest I do that though?"

Healer. "You could imagine yourself turning the tap on more that supplies those nutrients, so that it flows in the blood supply passing through your liver. That way every part becomes rejuvenated. Do you want to try that?"

Barry.   "A good idea, and I've turned the tap on fuller already. I can imagine it flowing and being taken up by my liver - I can imagine it becoming more active and really healthy looking now thank you."

Note. This treatment method may call for repetition.

BURNS AND SCALDS

These may be considered as the exposure of bodily parts to excessive heat and causing injury to the tissue. Burns and scalds may have any of many causes. Flame and dry heat causes burning, as can acids, alkalis, electricity, radiated energy, friction, sunlight rays and, seemingly paradoxically, by extreme cold such as from dry ice. Scalds result from hot water, hot vapour or steam.

The amount of the severity of the injury is referred to as the 'degree', and

these degrees vary from:
First degree, the colour change and congestion of the skin; but with no tissue destruction.

The second degree is where blistering occurs.

In the third degree, surface tissue becomes destroyed, and considerable shock is experienced together with significant pain.

In the fourth degree burn, both skin and underlying tissue becomes destroyed.

In the fifth degree burn, muscle tissue becomes destroyed.

In the six degree an entire limb becomes charred and disorganised.

The more the burning or scolding the more the shock will be experienced, and the degree of shock will be more related to the size of the area affected rather than it's penetration of damage. Indeed the shock factor is of major importance. Burns can cause toxin and bacterial invasion, higher temperatures, pulse rates and delirium can also occur, as well as collapse.

A BURN OR SCALDING TREATMENT METHOD

In all but the more minor cases medical treatment is urgently required, and in what follows are the healing methods to follow such treatment. The initial approach should always be to release any residual subconscious shock. This should be conducted along the lines of taking the subject back to the original accident using hypnosis, and encouraging the subject to describe his experience and the emotion he felt.

Having done this, the treatment method is to be directed at speeding the recovery of the damaged or painful part. (In the more minor cases, causing only discomfort, healing may be commenced directly. In the more minor cases we have more of an inconvenience or discomfort, and relief is required to quicken the resolution of a temporary situation. Given these circumstances the effects can be rapid.)

A SERIOUS BURN SCOLDING
HEALING EXAMPLE

At his home on bonfire night Frank had tripped whilst carrying three large mugs of scolding hot tea to his guests. In doing so he had scolded his left hand, but worse still, he was to fall with his extended right arm and hand into the red hot burning base of the fire, with the right sleeve of his plastic anorak being melted onto his wrist in the process.

He had been dragged free by his guests, shocked by Frank's screams and the suddenness with which it had happened. Frank had acted in a delirious state, and an ambulance had been called, which following immediate medical care by the crew, took him to casualty for emergency treatment.

Now Frank, unable to use his hands, urgently needs further assistance to speed his recovery. Frank also displays involuntary arm movements and is given to trembling since the accident. Frank has had his role explained, taken into hypnosis, and is sitting holding both arms out vertically from his elbows.

Healer. "As I explained Frank, we need to find out if your subconscious is still suffering from the shock of your accident. So I need to ask it some questions, and when I do here's how it responds. When the answer to a question is 'no', then your subconscious causes you to see red, or perhaps a red light to come on - rather like a red traffic light. When the answer is 'yes', it does the same, but in that case with green. Your subconscious gives you either colour immediately I finish my question. Subconscious, Frank, using those colours, are you still suffering shock from the accident?"

Frank. "It says 'yes', I saw a green light."

Healer. "Thank you subconscious. Subconscious, would it help to relieve you of that shock if Frank had a second opportunity to think through what happened?"

Frank "Green again!"

Healer. "O.K. Frank, I want you to go back to that night, to be there not here, and pick up from when you were carrying those tea mugs."

Frank. "I think I know something is going to happen, but I don't know how. I can see the tea glinting in the light from the fire which is sparking a lot."

Healer. "Keep going Frank. What happens next?"

Frank. "I've tripped - I'm falling - Ahhh! - Ahhh! - The tea has burnt

127

my hand - Ahhh! Ahhh! My hands burning in the fire." (Tears and significant hand, arm and bodily movements accompany the emotion being recalled. Following a pause to allow the emotions to 'drain' from his subconscious, Frank is asked if he can continue.)

Frank.   "Yes, I can feel the agony, people are screaming - so am I. They're dragging me away and I feel completly disorientated - I know I'm in shock and I'm shouting, but I don't know what."

Healer.   "What happens next?"

Frank   "I keep fainting and coming back, the pain is sheer agony. People are running about - ugh! - someone has thrown water over my hands."

Healer.   "What happens next?"

Frank.   "The ambulance men are here, their bright light is hurting my eyes. I don't know what they're doing but I think I've been injected and they're talking to me but I can't think straight to answer them."

Healer.   "What happens next?"

Frank.   "I'm on a stretcher in the ambulance, the siren is going and I can see the flashing blue lights being reflected. The journey seems rough and bumpy. But the pain is easing and I'm feeling a bit better but worried about what has happened to me."

Healer.   "And what happens next Frank?"

Note. Following this Frank reported his experiences on reaching the hospital, the treatment he had had, and how he'd reacted on leaving and going home. Having been highly emotional during this stage of thetherapy, and reporting feeling 'drained' by it, it was decided to defer the physical healing for two days later. Upon his return he was reminded of his role, taken into hypnosis and the second stage of treatment commenced, with Frank seeming noticeably much better than on his first visit.

Healer.   "OK. Frank, which hand and wrist do you want to work on first?"

Frank.   "I'm not bothered about my left - it's my right hand - and the wrist where they had to remove the melted plastic from my anorak sleeve."

Healer.   "O.K. then, what comes first, shall we work down from your wrist?"

Frank. "Yes, I want to do that first."

Healer. "Then, with your eyes remaining shut, I want you to imagine yourself looking at it, and tell me what you are drawn too."

Frank. "I know what it looks like and I'm imagining myself looking at that. It's a mess, it's wrinkled, scarred, all sorts of nasty colours and it looks awful."

Healer. "O.K. What should we try first?"

Frank. "Well, it's the skin that needs help - could we do something about that?"

Healer. "Yes, we could see ourselves replacing the damaged skin with healthy new skin."

Frank. "Yes that's the only way to treat this - but how should I do that?"

Healer. "Could you imagine yourself working on it like they do with broken and uneven paving stone paths? When they do this they remove the old blocks, section by section, level and make good the foundations, and then lay a lovely even new surface - do you want to try that sort of approach?"

Frank. "Yes. I can imagine that, I'll start from where it's healthy and work down, but it's broken and uneven skin I shall see myself replacing."

Healer. "Right, begin to start the replacements and tell me what's happening as you do."

Frank. "I'm lifting each bit like a thick flake, I'll do a few rows at a time, clean the underneath and then fill it to make it nice and even, then I'll lay a new skin tile and tap each into place and fill in the gaps with liquid skin. I'm starting that now - but it will take time."

Healer. "O.K. Frank, but keep me informed as you go."

Note. Frank reports a series of such replacements until he reaches the point where his wrist joins his hand. Following this Frank sees himself doing the same with his hand. Frank then reports that he can imagine it all looking good, and just as his hand and wrist looked like before the accident.

Healer. "I'd like you to imagine your wrist and hand being supplied with

129

special   healthy nutrients to support the return to perfect health in those parts, how could you imagine doing that?"

Frank.   "I could put some into the blood stream so it would seep out, and I could ease it in with my finger tips from the outside."

Healer.   "Excellent idea, do that and tell me what happens as you do."

Frank.   "Well, internally I've opened a valve to release the special nutrients into the blood stream, and I can imagine it soaking into the tissues and reaching the skin area. Now I'm putting some onto the skin with my fingers. It seems soothing and fresh. It's all done now."

Healer.   "Does anything else need attention for the rapid recovery to become complete?"

Frank.   "No, only a little time for it all to set."

Healer.   "Good, without actually moving your wrist and hand I'd like you to imagine yourself watching it moving, smoothly comfortably and naturally, and just as it did before."

Frank.   "Yes, I've done that, it looks good."

Healer.   "Good, now actually make some movements and tell me how it feels."

Frank.   "That's amazing. It's freer and far more comfortable - I'm quite surprised."

Note. Frank next works on his left hand using a similar procedure, and is invited to return for a further enhancement of the healing the following week. Upon his return he reports feeling very much better mentally, and physically. His skin is visibly healing very well too. During this visit a further visualisation of skin healing by applying nutrients and creams takes place.

A MINOR BURN TREATMENT METHOD

In these cases hypnosis is normally unnecessary, and the treatment method can not only be remarkably simple, but rapid too. This lends the treatment to public demonstration, to the relief of attending subjects distracted by discomfort, and by no means least, to help inspire confidence in the Healer's abilities.

Among the more common example are ladies who recently accidentally 'caught' themselves whilst ironing, a subject who has 'burned' the joint between thumb and finger opening a bottle top, or touched the lighted end of a cigarette as examples. In such cases it is mostly sufficient for the Healer to hold a hand, or to 'cup' both over the affected area - but without physical contact.

Although warmth will be mostly experienced by the subject during the process, subject's seldom if ever report that this adds to any discomfort felt from the residual 'heat' of the original burning, the warmth being of a healing and comforting nature instead. In a like manor to this simple burn treatment method, small cuts, grazes and 'hurt' fingers and skin areas can be similarly treated. Little further by way of explanation is required, but for completion a healing example follows.

A MINOR BURN OR SCOLD
TREATMENT EXAMPLE

Jan. has 'caught' the small finger side of her right hand on a cooker ring she was unaware to be switched on. Technically she has received a 'first degree' burn, but regards it as no more than distracting discomfort which has prevented her from freely using her hand. Following the Healer's request for her to hold her hand forward, the Healer is standing cupping his hands an inch or so away from her hand.

Healer. "O.K. Jan, just stay like this for a moment or two, and let me know if you feel anything happening."

Jan. (After a pause) "Yes, it's feeling warm, but not in a way that it adds to the burn, more comforting."

Healer. "Good, that's the healing taking place."

Jan. (A few moments later) "I do believe it's feeling easier, yes it is."

Healer. "Good, just a little longer and the healing will then just continue by itself."

Jan. "Yes it does feel better."

Healer. "O.K., I'll take my hands away and see what it looks like now."

Jan. "Oh! The reds nearly gone, and it feels quite comfortable now, thank you."

HEART ATTACKS

Medically referred to as Heart Failure, and a general term referring to the disability of the heart to maintain a healthy circulation.

In this the heart's muscles weaken or fail, or the rhythm of the stimulation of the heart is affected, and a reduced blood flow results. Many causes are known of, including heart muscles weakened by toxaemia, over exertion, heart blockage and infection for examples.

However, a strong indication of a link between some heart failures and psychological factors cannot be dismissed, and in my opinion are common contributory causes, especially following shock. Various names are given for heart conditions, and the attending subject will have had his condition diagnosed as one of them. However, it is beyond the co text of this book to cover in any detail the extensive research knowledge and experience that modern medicine has in this area.

HEART FAILURE

As previously referred to, heart failure is a term used to describe the hearts reduced capacity to maintain an adequate circulation, it can develop gradually, leading to a reduction in the ability to perform physical activity without discomfort. This can result from the reduced abilities of the heart muscles, from irregularities of the stimulation of the hearts rhythm, reduced contractions of the heart muscles or the slowing of the hearts activity resulting in a reduced circulation.

The heart may be weakened by toxins or by a reduced blood supply. Insufficiency of blood may occur during excessive exertion, particularly in cases of narrowed or leaking heart valves. The heart's efficiency may also be reduced by drugs. Medically heart failure is referred to as either acute or chronic.

ACUTE HEART FAILURE

The most common cause of this condition is coronary artery thrombosis. The symptoms are severe pains in the chest area, which are also often felt in the left arm. Palpitations, breathlessness and unconsciousness can result. The onset may be sudden, but often some symptoms will have been noticed prior to the attack.

CHRONIC HEART FAILURE

The most common causes of the more general gradual reductions in the heart's capacity to circulate blood are:

1.The disease of blood vessels.

2.Disruption or disturbance of the heart rhythm.

3.Increased pressure caused by chronic bronchitis, emphysema and pulmonary fibrosis.

4.Systemic circulation pressures due to arteriosclerosis or chronic nephritis (kidney inflammation).

5.'Mechanical' effects such as the presence of a tumour. In this fifth cause, symptoms can include increasing breathlessness on exertion, palpitations and oedema (the abnormal accumulation of water fluid in bodily parts).

ANGINA PECTORIS

Mostly a condition of middle aged men and experienced as severe chest pain, which can also be experienced in the arms, particularly the left. These pains are experienced either during or immediately following physical activity, and causes such activity to cease. A sense of pending demise is commonly experienced by the victim. However the symptoms normally pass off in a few minutes or so.

Angina is itself a symptom rather than a disease, and implying that the heart's muscle is receiving insufficient oxygen - often because of arteriosclerosis of the coronary arteries. The indications of psychological factors are often to be found playing a part.

A TREATMENT METHOD FOR HEART FAILURE

The treatment method is to follow conventional medical treatment, and to go hand-in-hand with on-going medical supervision and assistance rather than seeking to replace either. A psychological connection, either as a cause or contributing factor should be sought for. Additionally, the subject's subconscious should be called upon to indicate the location of the physiological area for treatment, and be requested to indicate which of the causes, given in the previous description of heart failure text require attention. Following this approach the actual treatment is proceeded with.

A HEART FAILURE TREATMENT EXAMPLE

Richard has been diagnosed as suffering with arteriosclerotic heart disease. His doctor and heart specialist suspect the cause to be his heavy smoking, and he has been warned of the risk of a coronary attack. He has received dietary advice and been told to exercise more, but above all to stop smoking. Richard doesn't feel too bad in himself, and his condition only came to light following a medical examination for a life insurance policy.

However, Richard is now most concerned, and originally visited for assistance to give up his smoking. Richard has accepted the idea that it would be best for the anti-smoking therapy to follow his heart therapy, when any psychological factors had been resolved. Richard has had his role explained to him and is relaxed into hypnosis.

Healer. "Subconscious, Richard has reported to me that his Doctor has diagnosed him to have a condition affecting his heart. Subconscious, shortly I will help you to help Richard with this, and to do so I need some   assistance from you. Richard is most concerned about his condition, so that when I ask you 'yes' or 'no' questions to help me, here's how you respond. When the answer to a question is 'yes', you cause Richard to see green,   perhaps like a green lawn or a green traffic light, or just cause him to have his mind think green. When I ask you a question and the answer to that is a 'no', you do the same thing but that time by using red. Perhaps a red traffic light, a red flower or just having Richard think red. So green for 'yes' and red for 'no', and you make the appropriate colour unmistakably dominant. Subconscious, using those two colours, I want you to carry out a thorough exam-ination of Richard's circulation system in his chest area and signal green when you have completed the examination.

Richard. (20 seconds later.) "Green, yes I've got a green dot in my mind".

Healer   "Good, subconscious, do you find that area of Richard's circulation healthy and fit, yes or no?"

Richard. "No! I've got a red dot".

Healer. "Subconscious, is that area unfit because of Richard's smoking?"

Richard. "I've got both dots now."

Healer. "Subconscious, are you saying that Richard's smoking has played a part but there is also some other factor or factors?"

Richard. "I've got a large green dot now."

Healer "Thank you subconscious, I'll count to three, click my fingers and you cause Richard to realise what that additional factor is. One, two three 'click'.

Richard. "It's what I've been eating - I can see my food."

Healer. "Subconscious, Richard has told me that he has been given dietary advice from his Doctor which Richard is sticking to exactly. Subconscious, given that, would the food factor diminish and go away?"

Richard. "I've got two green dots now!"

Healer. "Subconscious, is there a further factor or factors other than Richard's smoking and previous eating habits playing a part?"

Richard. "Green - yes."

Healer. "Then I'll count to three and click my fingers and you have Richard realise such a factor that contributes to his condition then. One two three 'click'"

Richard. "I don't know why, but I feel a bit angry - no, wait! I see it now, I've always been quick tempered and I often get very angry and stressed over things."

Healer. "Thank you for that information subconscious, is there a further factor contributing to Richard's condition?"

Richard. "I'm not sure, I get both red and green but neither is very clear."

Healer. "Subconscious, are you saying that the further factor is what caused Richard to suffer with anger?"

Richard. "Yes, green."

135

Healer.   "Richard has decided to go through analysis with me to release his stress and anger. When this has been done would there be any further factor contributing to Richard's condition?"

Richard. "No, I've got a red dot."

Healer.   "Thank you subconscious, now Richard knows what needs to be done, would you be prepared to ease Richard's condition whilst the analysis takes place - which is to be followed by the therapy to help Richard stop smoking?"

Richard. "Two green dots two - yes, yes!"

Following this, the treatment method given for arteriosclerosis is preceded with, and to be repeated following analysis and the smoking cessation therapy.

A SECOND TREATMENT METHOD
FOR HEART FAILURE

Jane reports that she suffered what her Doctor's have described as acute heart failure. This attack had come on suddenly whilst she was asleep in the night.

She had experienced severe pain and breathlessness, and had been rushed to the casualty department of her General Hospital. Despite the intensive medical care she has received she is still suffering from pains, reduced activity and significant anxiety. Her condition has been caused by coronary thrombosis and her specialist also suspects the possibility of a slightly faulty heart valve.

During the examination procedure conducted in a similar way to that set out for Richard, in the Heart Failure Treatment Example, the stress experienced in her early childhood as an orphaned foster child was revealed to be the main causual factor. She had been placed with several families, not all of which had been good to her. This had lead to a lack of confidence, anxiety and a severe sense of insecurity and self dislike.

A similar procedure was again adopted as that given for Richard - except that Jane neither smoked nor had a bad dietary habits. However, during the analysis the heart valve that was suspected of being faulty was to be treated, and the healing proceeded as follows, with Jane in hypnosis and understanding her role.

Healer. "O.K. Jane, I want you to imagine yourself down there and looking at those valves, and tell me what you imagine yourself seeing."

Jane. "I'm thinking of a tube with a flap inside, like a tube with a small toilet seat cover."

Healer. "Good, look at them one at a time and tell me if you notice any thing."

Jane. "Yes, I'm doing that - I think one needs repairing."

Healer. "O.K. Tell me what needs to be done."

Jane. "I don't know, but I'm imagining that the flap is a bit stiff and too big for the tube."

Healer. "Shall we tackle the size matters first?"

Jane. "Yes, but how?"

Healer. "Well, we could either imagine the tube being enlarged, the flap being made smaller - or both."

Jane. "Yes, let's do both - but how should I do it?"

Healer. "Well could you clean the edges of the flap of any corrosion or surplus tissue, and then imagine yourself enlarging the tube a bit in some way - like moulding it out a little, as if it were made from soft pliable plasticine, by using your little finger?"

Jane. "Yes, that's a good idea. I'll start by running my nail file around the edges of the flap - I can see it as if it's sort of caked and gritty around the edges."

Healer. "Tell me when you've done that Jane."

Jane. (A few moments later.) "Yes, I've done that and it looks clean and smooth now."

Healer. "Good, now see yourself widening the tube in some way and keep me in touch with your progress."

Jane.   "I'm using my little finger, pushing it in and turning it a little each way - it's getting larger, my finger fits in easily now."

Healer.   "Excellent, is it large enough now then?"

Jane.   Yes, it looks alright now."

Healer.   "O.K. Jane now look at that flap coming down and tell me how it fits."

Jane.   "It fits well enough, but it seems stiff - the hinge needs oiling I think."

Healer.   "How can you do that?"

Jane   "I'll use my small oil dropper that I use with my sewing machine - that will take it."

Healer.   "Good, tell me how it goes."

Jane.   "That's done it, it fits perfectly and it's free to move properly.

Note. Following this a similar approach was made with each remaining valve.

Next Jane was treated for her thrombosis, and in a similar way as given for cerebral thrombosis. Subsequently Jane also attended for analysis.

A TREATMENT METHOD EXAMPLE
FOR WEAKENED HEART MUSCLES

David has reported that his heart was weakened during an illness he suffered two years previously. (Rheumatic fever, for example, can cause such results.) David has undergone the examination procedure and no other causual factor than his illness has been discovered. His subconscious has agreed that it would be possible to strengthen his heart. David is in hypnosis and understands his role.

Healer.   "Imagine you can see your heart David, and tell me what you imagine it looks like."

David.   "It's not firm, it seems too small and a bit shrivelled."

Healer.   "What do you need to treat first?"

138

David. "Well it's all the same problem, my heart needs a stimulating sort of exercise or massaged in some way I think."

Healer. "How could you do that then?"

David. "Goodness knows, but that's what's needed though."

Healer. "How about your turning a tap on somewhere to release strengthening nutrient into that part, so that it soaks into the muscles and fills them out and strengthens them?"

David. "Yes, that's a good idea - I can feel it needs that tonic, sort of re-inflating."

Healer. "Good, do that and tell me how it goes."

David. I can see two taps, and I'm turning both on now. One tap is for the tonic and the other one is for strengthening nourishment - there's plenty of both."

Healer. "Now that you've done that, what's happening to the heart?"

David. "It's filling out, getting larger and firmer - it's looking better too."

Healer. "Keep going David until it looks right."

David. (A little later.) "That's it, I think."

Healer. "Why does something tell you more needs to be done?"

David. "Yes, there's something missing I sense, but I don't know what."

Healer. "Could it be that it needs some kind of massage to make sure that there are no airlocks or parts not filled with the tonic and nourishment?"

David. "Yes, - I got that green light again. I think that if I gently squeeze it a bit, and work it with the palms of my hands that will do the trick nicely."

Healer. "O.K. Then do that and keep me in touch with your progress."

David. "That's doing it - I feel better, warmer and my breathing seems easier too."

PART EIGHT

TREATING MIND CONDITIONS

STRESS

Stress can express itself in a wide range of human reactions, and these can include undue over reactions, fear, hate, tempers, anger, rages, frustration, poor sleep, lack of concentration, unpredictability and reduced motivation. More commonly stress will show itself as anxiety. Bodily functions may also be affected, trembling, poor digestion, and in some cases by the additional factors of increased alcohol and tobacco consumption. A depletion of vitamin B often occurs, and this should be supplemented with vitamin B Complex on advice. Relationship difficulties, work, financial worry, tension pressure from responsibilities and insecurity can all be factors.

Once stress takes effect contributing factors may combine, or be drawn in by the sufferer's generally deteriorated attitudes towards other situations.

In modern society stress is a major concern, although it can be argued that in one form or another it has probably been with us throughout our history, though it may justifiably be said that it is now more common and openly conspicuous. Road Rage is an example of this more modern aspect. Stress is a psychosomatic condition which can lead to neurosis. Physical symptoms and many illnesses have it as their basic causes. High blood pressure, headaches, palpitations, coronary thrombosis, mental pains, skin rashes and infertility are common examples.

STRESS TREATMENT

Treating stress calls for two approaches. The identification and attempted resolution of it's cause, and secondly, especially where little prospects exist of a change of the causual factors, for the sufferer to seek to alter his attitude and reaction to such factors. By it's very nature, stress will alter the viewpoint of the sufferer who, in many cases, could be helped in considering appropriate stress reducing changes by seeking advice from an intelligent trustworthy friend.

As an example, I was once consulted by a male client who reported he drank excessively to cope with his stress from his work. When we analysed his situation it appeared that he worked where he did because of his good wages. Calculating what he was spending on alcohol, and deducting that from his earnings, it emerged that he was not only suffering stress and the adverse effects from his drinking caused by his occupation, but that he was actually financially worse off than he would have been from a lower paid job that would end his source related stress by being much easier to cope with. In this case he changed his occupation, gave up his drinking and began to enjoy his life far more fully.

Unfortunately not all stress causes can be resolved by variations, changes and action taking. Where little can be done, the second approach requires attempting. That is the attitude towards the causual factor needs to be changed. In this second approach it should first be realised that stress is often brought on by ourselves, that is the mental approach or reaction we have to a given situation. As such, understandable as it is, stress is the result of attitude.

Although stress can be 'catching', often only one or a few people in a similar situation will suffer it, when this is the case clearly attitudes must vary. As a much simplified example of differing reactions based upon attitude, consider two men in a pub. Each has in front of him a pint glass, each containing a remaining half pint of beer. To the man who is an excessive drinker his glass is already half empty. To the other who rather dislikes drinking, his glass is still half full.

I once visited a large D.I.Y. store, the public address was in constant use, calling for various people to answer a phone call or to attend some location in the store. This not only distracted me but quickly made me feel annoyed by it's intrusion on my thinking. Seeing a smiling assistant I asked her how she coped with it all day. She seemed quite surprised that I should ask her that. Smiling again she replied "but it's good, it shows what a busy place this is and I enjoy my job and being busy."

141

In a similar way we might avoid some restaurant which plays constant music, but then enjoy visiting some night club where the music is so loud that shouting is needed to be heard.

A TREATMENT METHOD FOR STRESS

Firstly being relaxed in hypnosis is an essential prerequisite.

Secondly a caring sympathetic and trustworthy second person should be in attendance. These may be referred to as Healer and subject respectively. The Healer, in approximately one hour long sessions, is to encourage the subject to talk freely about the factors producing his stress. In this the Healer is to offer no advice, be in anyway critical of the subject nor raise issues that the subject might consider controversial - such as the healer asking "then why not divorce her?"

The sessions are to be on going at approximately weekly intervals. During these sessions, and the time span between them, a gradual draining away of the tension from the stress producing attitude can be expected to occur, with approximately eight such sessions held in all.

This remarkably simple approach, referred to as analysis, can work wonders, as the case history to follow illustrates. If the subject can be brought to find a previous negative experience to be funny and laugh at it in hypnosis, dramatic mental attitude changes can result.

A male client attended suffering acute stress reporting, "I'm on the verge of a complete breakdown and I've been laid off sick by my doctor. My wife has been threatening to leave me and if she does I shall commit suicide."

Following the treatment method of analysis given, he attended his last session. On arrival I asked how he was, 'fine' he replied. Enthusiastically I asked about his wife. For a moment he seemed a little suprised that I should ask, then dismissed the subject as of no importance, saying that his marriage was much better. Immediately he continued by saying. "No, what's really important is a great new job I've just been offered".

BLOW AWAYS

This is an amazingly good, and often instant method of resolving some attitude or feeling towards an experience or situation. The subject in hypnosis with his eyes closed, is to create a mental picture to represent some concern.

Having done that he is to imagine himself blowing that picture away. Two or more attempts may be required. The action is a highly successful method of instructing the intermediate subconscious mind that it should no longer be concerned with the issue. Any scene chosen by the client will suit the purpose. He may for example, imagine himself blowing some person away - perhaps through a wall.

He may blow away a place, building or location, or blow himself away. This exercise has to be tried for it's effectiveness to be believed.

MYALGIC ENCEPHALOMYELITIS (M.E.) AND MULTIPLE SCLEROSIS (M.S.)

These two separate conditions have been linked together since the healing attempt is similar for both. In my experience as an Holistic Hypnotherapist both have been found to have similar causes, but with each developing it's own symptom or condition. The basic cause for both arises because the sufferer situation.

In M.E. this mental over taxation produces a form of lacking strength, energy, enthusiasm and physical ability. Additional symptoms can include short temperedness, pain behind the eyes, bodily aching, sore throat, higher temperatures and extended sleeping. The condition is often called, somewhat unkindly, 'yuppie flue' since it more commonly effects younger career orientated men.

However, the condition also effects females, but here too mostly with those who might be described as 'achievers', or those under pressure from themselves or others to achieve promotion or success in their occupations and professions. As such M.E. could be regarded as the mind disabling the sufferer in order to cause him to slow-up or even to opt out of the mental pressures sustained, clearly though, in a way that the victim cannot be blamed for doing so.

Additionally the victim is unlikely to view it that way, and instead repeatedly feel and report his frustration and even anger at seeing himself restricted or 'losing out'. In this condition the intermediate subconscious mind has sought relief from it's pressures by seeking to prevent or restrict further mental loading.

In Multiple Sclerosis a similar situation is often to be found, but sometimes the result is directly linked with an event which has then ceased, or be a reflection of a situation of the past. In the case of M.S. there is a disease of the nervous system, the cause of which is unknown medically. The condition is usually a progressive one, although temporary remissions can occur. The condition can produce weakness, poor co-ordination, rigidity and paralysis of the legs, arm tremor and effect speech.

THE TREATMENT FOR M.E. AND M.S.

The Healer is to take the subject into hypnosis and then encourage the subject to talk to the Healer openly and without inhibition. The Healer is to listen and encourage the subject to talk about every aspect of his life - especially going back over his earliest memories. The Healer is to avoid criticising, advising or suggesting that the subject has misunderstood some experience.

The Healer's role is to be confined to sympathetically encouraging the subject to talk and express his emotions freely. Such sessions should each be for one hours duration, and take place no more frequently than five days apart, and a gap of more than ten days should be avoided. Eight to fifteen sessions may well be required to complete the course. This analysis approach is similar to psychotherapy, but combined with hypnosis the therapy is greatly speeded.

HOW THE HEALING METHOD WORKS

During the procedure, and in hypnosis, the subject gains a greater capacity to exercise his subconscious mind in a way little else can equal, and during the course of the sessions release trapped emotions and repressed experiences. Without the subject being consciously aware of it, each memory or event he talks about will, in hypnosis, trigger an extended reaction in the subject's subconscious, even with seemingly non important or 'silly' matters.

A comparison, for further understanding the process, would be to think of a tree. It is as if the subject can see the tree's trunk at the conscious level, but not the branches above, which can be thought of at the subconscious level. When the subject talks of one matter it is as if the branch of his mind dealing with it fans out in its thinking, and then along the smaller branches and twigs of the original branch holding the memory or subject being talked about by the subject.

Further to this, it is also as if further branches develop and penetrate further into the memories and emotions within the subconscious.

Consequently, with trapped emotions becoming encountered, it is as if those twigs and branches now act to conduct trapped emotions to the conscious mind level - where they can be resolved. In this way the harmful emotions that lay behind M.E. and M.S. cease to have their effect or purpose. In short a discharge of the mental anxiety has occurred.

THE IRRITABLE BOWEL SYNDROME (I.B.S.)

In this condition any of a wide range of symptoms may occur. Commonly these can include stomach discomfort, severe stomach pains (sometimes referred to as migraine stomach), constipation, diarrhoea, nausea, anxiety, appetite loss, incontinence, vomiting, depression, moodiness, irritability, frequent urination and digestive problems.

Many victims will be severely restricted in their social lives and their freedom to travel. The ability to follow their occupations is also impeded in some cases.

A COMMON CAUSE OF I.B.S.

A common cause of I.B.S. is the reaction to what is known as the 'Flight or Fight Response'. This is a further interesting quality or ability of the subconscious, and when triggered it can make us immensely physically stronger. The extra strength may express itself in many ways, with people able to achieve superhuman feats of physical ability. This increased ability is in itself only part of the effect of the flight or fight response. The response can also trigger many other reactions within us as part of it. The basic principle of the response is to enable us to be at our physical best to deal with a significant perceived danger.

Imagine, by way of explanation, that you came across a tiger in a forest about to attack you. You perceive your survival by escaping or facing it to fight it in some way. The subconscious mind goes onto full alert and adjusts the body for its maximum potential. Instantly the liver produces extra glucose for energy and strength, extra oil is secreted so that under a greater than normal load the muscle fibres will glide more freely over each other; air intake rises and quite likely, the subconscious may also be inclined to empty the digestive system to save oxygen. If it does you may urinate, defecate or vomit. (When we recall how lacking in energy we can be following a meal, it is obvious that in such an emergency the consumption of energy, particularly oxygen for digestion, is a luxury that cannot be afforded).

It is for this reason that the digestive tract can be spontaneously emptied in such an emergency. Many people have experienced feeling sick during some dramatic event, or even by just feeling nervous lost their appetite, needed to urinate and breathed more deeply or felt their stomach tighten. The flight or fight response of the mind is designed for relatively short-term emergencies and as such serves us well.

If however the origin of a flight or fight response is not to the tiger in a forest, but to some unresolved psychological emotive anxiety, then a version of this response may continue indefinitely to some degree, or alternatively it may recur each time as an experience, similar to the original cause, once again occurs. That is until in hypnosis the active ingredient of the memory is passed back to the conscious mind through analysis, where it can be resolved.

A TREATMENT METHOD FOR I.B.S.

A remarkable successful treatment method for I.B.S. is to take the subject into hypnosis and encourage him to talk about himself and his experiences of life. Such sessions, being of an hours duration and repeated weekly for some eight to ten weeks, helps the subject become once again aware of the experience lying behind the subconscious anxiety creating the I.B.S. symptoms, and to resolve the original issue.

Later in the sessions, say in session seven, the process of recall can often be concluded by the healer telling the subject's subconscious that it is recalling and remembering what happened to cause the subject's I.B.S. this statement being given three times is then followed by the healer saying, "in a moment I shall count to three, click my fingers and you will be back there at a time when something was happening, or about to happen, which directly lead to your I.B.S. problem. One, two, three 'click!'"

PANIC ATTACKS

A panic attack occurs when the subconscious reacts to an earlier event when a subsequent similar incident, experience, environmental situation, object, thought, picture, suggestion or concept is encountered, which reminds the subconscious of similarities with that previous experience, and one that resulted in traumatic consequences. With subsequent experiences, the triggering point will often broaden out, so that what begins with a reaction to one situation results in similar reactions to others.

In the panic attack, the victim has a profound and almost uncontrollable

146

urge to get away from, or in some way escape from a situation others would see as acceptable. In the panic attack, the subject also sees the demonstrated reaction as illogical and inexplicable to himself, as much as it is to others. During the attack the subconscious will take over the person's reactions, or attempt to do so. The victim is greatly alarmed and may sweat, tremble, have a racing heartbeat, breathe heavily yet feel oxygen starved, he may feel he is about to pass out, become uncontrollable or hysterical. The desire, brought on by the fear, to escape or avoid some situation becomes all but overwhelming, and almost nothing is too high a price to pay for the escape.

The fear of flying may develop into panic attacks in which, rather than remain seated, it becomes as if the subconscious would rather have him jump out of the aircraft, even at thirty thousand feet. However, in less restrictive circumstances, a victim may be at great risk of actual harm as the result of an attempt to escape while the intelligent mind is temporarily overruled by the subconscious illiminating logic. As if with a perverse mental reaction, instead of attempting to flee, the victim might well feel fixed and rooted to the spot, be unable to move, actually collapse or simply react with frenzy. Panic attacks can produce the greatest physical and mental reactions to be found in humans.

Panic attacks are common, not rare, and the victim will go to great lengths, to avoid them and make enormous efforts to fight them.

A TREATMENT METHOD FOR PANIC ATTACKS

The subject is taken into hypnosis and encouraged to talk about his memories, experiences and himself. During the eight-to-ten one hour weekly sessions the subject will once again be able to recall the repressed event or experience which originally created the anxiety causing his panic attacks. The process can often be greatly enhanced by the healer, in session seven, saying to the subject's subconscious three times, "subconscious (subject's name) you are recalling and remembering what has happened to (subject's name) to cause him to have his panic attacks. In a moment I shall count to three, click my fingers and you pass that memory back to (client's name). One, two, 'click'."

MIGRAINE

At one time I was a victim. The pain of this normally horrendous condition is probably brought about by blood pressure in brain veins. The attacks can be frequent or widely spaced. Many sufferers will, in their desperation, experiment with diet, avoid conditions or situations they feel bring the attacks on, and become prepared to attempt almost any form of relief or partial relief, that can be gained.

In some, and given time, its severity will reduce and in the lucky ones, eventually disappear, although possibly at the expense of some replacement symptom appearing sooner or later. The symptoms vary widely both in their intensity and type, but commonly distortions of vision and an aversion to light precede and then accompany the fearful head pains. Nausea, appetite loss, debility, lack of concentration, loss of energy, demoralisation, unsociability, withdrawal and other symptoms are common.

In the more severe cases cluster migraine may emerge, in which the agony is not focused at one point, but is felt more as if the head contained a grape like bunch, with each grape a centre of pain. Victims may bang their own heads in exasperation and frustration. In fact migraine can produce the highest level of pain experienced by humans.

One method of coping with migraine is to intensely concentrate on some interesting subject, especially if constructive or potentially rewarding. Given sufficient concentration, especially to detail, the mind become distracted from the anxiety producing the migraine, bringing relief. Great works of art and inventions are often thought to have been the results of this alleviation method.

Some of history's most famous people are thought to have had their inspirations as a distraction from this and other agonies. To a far more modest extent I did this myself, resulting in the largest and mot successful carpentry project I ever attempted. Fortunately too, migraine is highly responsive to analysis, following which the condition can be expected to be permanently removed. In every case I have come across, migraine, in whatever form, has proved to be the result of a repressed anxiety.

A TREATMENT METHOD FOR MIGRAINE

A very successful treatment of this condition is to take the subject into hypnosis and encourage him to talk about his memories, experiences and himself. During the eight-to-ten one hour sessions, and spaced at weekly intervals, his subconscious mind will, in most cases, begin to become increasingly aware of the original experience which caused the suppressed anxiety producing his migraine attacks. When this experience is recalled and resolved by his awareness of it, the migraine will in some cases be greatly reduced in its effects, and in even more cases cease altogether.

During session seven the process may be enhanced by the healer repeating to the subject's subconscious, three times, "Subconscious (subject's name), you are recalling and remembering what has happened to cause (subject's name) migraine. In a moment, subconscious I shall count to three, click my fingers and you pass that memory to back to (subject's name) One, two, three 'click'!".

PART NINE

MAGNET THERAPY

MAGNETIC HEALING

Many diseases and organ functioning breakdowns are caused by electrochemical failures, which can result in cell mutation. It has been put forward that magnetic energy is our first line of defence, that is preventative, and our immune system our second line of defence, that is, a response after the cause of our ailment.

World wide over 100 million people already use this magnetic therapy, 30 million in Japan alone, where millions sleep on magnetic mattresses to alleviate the effects of the pain and stress of their lives, and to treat a whole variety of various mind and bodily conditions, by enhancing the body's ability to maintain and heal itself naturally.

Already firmly established, this healing method, which could be called magnet-therapy, must be destined to become a vital healing method. A major advantage is its simplicity, for example, to benefit one only has to lay on a specially designed magnetic mattress, or a mattress covering, or wear a magnet.

For those attracted by the concept of effortless self healing, surely nothing could be more appealing. Not least is the durability of the healing appliances to be considered, for once obtained they can provide years of beneficial effect.

150

It is beyond this work to provide the technical information of how these aids provide such remarkable results, suffice to say that, in simpler forms, they were in use by the ancient Egyptians long before their science could explain their function.

What can be said is that iron is an essential element to the human system - hence vitamin and iron tonics, iron tablets, and the stress laid on the beneficial iron content of many foods.
It was discovered in 1826 that our blood contains 4% iron, which is carried in the haemoglobin in the red blood corpuscles. It is logical, therefore, that blood is effected by magnetic fields.

Applying a magnet to blood creates a corkscrew-like turbulence. This increased activity in the blood stream improves blood circulation, and helps the blood to absorb more effectively cholesterol, toxins and other waste products that could normally lodge on the artery walls.

Improved circulation can make the hands and feet feel much warmer, helps prevent blocked arteries, and regenerates damaged tissue more quickly. This is due to an increase in the rate of which oxygen and nutrients are supplied to generate healthy new cells, and to flush waste products from the body.

With this healing method the blood is cleansed and eases the work load of the heart, and fatigue and pain can disappear. Junctions of the automatic nerves are normalised, so that the internal organs controlled by them regain their proper functions.

The secretions of hormones is promoted, with the result that the skin can gain lustre, youth is preserved, and ailments due to the lack of hormone secretion are relieved or cured. Blood and lymph circulations are activated, and because of this, nutrients are more easily and effectively carried to every cell in the body.

In turn, this helps in promoting metabolism in general. The magnetic waves invigorate body organs, providing an enhanced resistance to disease. These specially designed magnets can have significant beneficial effects on many conditions, such as toothache, joint stiffness, pains and swellings, cervical spondylits, eczema, asthma, chilblains, injuries and wounds.

Sleeping on a magnetised mattress can reduce or eliminate pain, promote sounder sleep, and generate greater day-time energy. Additionally, astounding effects on some serious illnesses have been reported. These, by way of example, have included: epilepsy, schizophrenia, chronic fatigue, depression and diabetes.

A very obvious and immediate strengthening effect of the magnets can easily be demonstrated - much to the surprise of those participating, by the following a simple experiment.

Bare footed the subject holds out his arms, with one hand on top of the other. A second person then pushes down on the subject's hands to lower the subject's arms, while the subject gently resists the pressure. With the combined weight of both sets of arms, and a little strength being applied, the subject's arms will inevitably be forced to descend. Next the subject is to stand on a magnetised surface, such as a pair of magnetic shoe liners, especially designed for magnet-therapy. The exercise explained is then repeated, and much to the surprise of both, the second person now finds a significantly greater effort is required to lower the subject's arms.

Today, rather than the early 'pot-luck', approach of the users thousands of years ago, the science of magnet-therapy has seen spectacular advances in the development of health restorative magnets and magnetisation. Leaving the user free to purchase the appropriate aid, and use it without having to understand its construction or how it works. With the healing methods put forward earlier, the combination of the two approaches offers hope to millions that is currently beyond comprehension or evaluation.

A question often asked is, 'is magnet-therapy safe?' Well, firstly the magnets produced for health benefits are specifically designed for that purpose, and with gentle magnetic strengths well within the natural tolerance of the body. Despite this though, some users can experience some initial discomfort because their bodies are removing toxins.

All living creatures have successfully evolved in the earth's magnetic force field. Then too, natural magnetisation occurs in lodestone, and we commonly use them in powered hand tools, household appliances and to generate electricity itself. Magnets are provided as toys for children, and used in a whole range of useful aids. In all of this no case of a magnet being harmful is known to the author, save to the case of a friend who came for healing, having dropped a heavy magnet on his foot. Having said this, certainly anyone using a heart pacemaker or similar, should consult his medical advisor prior to using them. Health ministries world wide have declared this therapy harmless, so users should feel safe and comfortable in applying the marvel for themselves.